Planning and Using
A Total
Personnel System

Planning and Using
A Total
Personnel System

Richard A. Kaumeyer, Jr.

VNR VAN NOSTRAND REINHOLD COMPANY
NEW YORK   CINCINNATI   TORONTO   LONDON   MELBOURNE

Van Nostrand Reinhold Company Regional Offices:
New York   Cincinnati

Van Nostrand Reinhold Company International Offices:
London   Toronto   Melbourne

Copyright © 1982 by Van Nostrand Reinhold Company

Library of Congress Catalog Card Number: 81-10317
ISBN: 0-442-21370-0

Manufactured in the United States of America

Published by Van Nostrand Reinhold Company
135 West 50th Street, New York, N.Y. 10020

Published simultaneously in Canada by Van Nostrand Reinhold Ltd.

15 14 13 12 11 10 9 8 7 6 5 4 3 2 1

Library of Congress Cataloging in Publication Data

Kaumeyer, Jr., Richard A.
    Planning and using a total personnel system.

    Includes index.
    1. Personnel management.   I. Title.
HF5549.K2833   658.3   81-10317
ISBN 0-442-21370-0   AACR2

To
Laura Anne, Richard August III,
and
Jonathan Elliott

PREFACE

This book is designed for managers and practitioners in the field. The suggestions and steps to implement the various personnel systems are not based on guesswork. They are the result of years of experience in working with the personnel activity in all of its aspects. It should be of value in all the major areas of personnel—benefits, compensation, employee relations, employment, training and development, etc.

It is deliberately not written in the traditional academic format with multiple quotations and references. The intent is not to provide research on what others have published. Too often, from personal experience, these sources have spent limited time, if any at all, actually in the field.

This, as many other practices, is changing rapidly, and the change will have a positive effect. People today want to learn from those who have experienced something firsthand, rather than read about it or hear about it from someone else. This is becoming a world requiring firsthand experience and a field tested background. Only by experience can a person truly probe the depths of a function.

There is little question that the entire area of personnel is increasing in importance. We are seeing the heads of personnel reporting at, or close to, the top of most progressive organizations. There is every indication that this trend will continue as more emphasis is placed on the management of human resources.

A large percentage of this increase in power has come from outside pressures. These include union activity, affirmative action, ERISA, and OSHA. Without these pressures, it would be many years before personnel would receive the status and power that it now has. Also, as legal decisions are continually rendered in these areas, the importance of a sophisticated personnel activity is accentuated.

Another issue that is coming into play is that of productivity. Labor is no longer a cheap commodity in most parts of the world. The emphasis on it being a resource is on the increase. There is a correlation between the attitude of the employees and the productivity of any organization. The over-used cliche about "people being the most important resource" is gaining recognition as being valid.

People are gaining importance in the organization at the same time the activities they perform are becoming harder to measure. We are going from a production/manufacturing society to a service-oriented one. While measures of activity on the production line are available, we have a long way to go in measuring the administrative functions that make up the bulk of the service area.

As personnel has increased in importance, so has the emphasis on personnel systems. In fact, personnel systems groups are often given top billing, along with compensation, employment, etc. Automation is one of the things that has brought about this emphasis on personnel systems. Since personnel people have not been noted for their computer expertise, a separate function and a set of skills has arisen.

Systems techniques that have been found useful in setting up and maintaining automation have also been found very useful in the manual areas of personnel. The concept of systems is seen in the manual areas of personnel as well as those that are automated. The combination of both manual and automated systems interface will improve the operation of any department, and personnel is no exception.

The expansion of the concept of personnel systems is being seen in a number of areas. It is gaining a professional recognition outside of individual organizations. Clubs and professional groups are being formed that enhance both the status and the communication among those in the field. The concepts are also being taught in seminars as a body of knowledge. This has provided additional recognition and structure to the various systems concepts.

This book should be of use to those who want to set up a personnel system. It may also prove of value to those who have an established personnel systems group. At the very least, it allows an established group to think through their daily activities as viewed through the eyes of another. This type of reflection can often stir the creative process.

Many illustrations are included. They are designed to support the concept that a "picture is worth a thousand words." In many cases, they are not technical in nature, but are diagrams to augment or further explain the reading.

This book was written because there is a broad range of interest in the topic of personnel systems. Managers, supervisors, practitioners, students of business, and others all have contact with the topic at one time or another. Not only were liberal illustrations provided to aid this broad range of readers, but technical jargon has been avoided. In this way, it was hoped to provide a book of value to those practicing in the area, as well as those who would like to know a little more about the subject.

A constant theme repeats itself throughout. This deals with the fact that a "make or buy" decision exists in almost every facet of personnel systems today. In almost every instance, an entire personnel system or the various individual piece parts can be purchased from an outside vendor/consultant as well as made. The reason for this repetition is that busy professionals frequently turn only to a specific section of a book for reference. At a given point in time, they are interested in a specific portion of the subject matter. The concept of "make or buy" is too important to be mentioned in only one section, since it should be part of any personnel systems decision.

Too many organizations limit themselves to just one choice. This can range from designing only one system to using only one vendor/consultant. In both cases, this leaves extremely limited options for the organization.

There are many companies today that have waited years for a new personnel system that seems never to arrive, as well as those that have waited for years for a system modification to a portion of the personnel system that also seems never to arrive. In most cases, the reason this happens is that they have erroneously limited their options to make or buy.

All areas of activity are moving faster in this rapidly changing world. Organizations may need a personnel system or a modification almost immediately. If their make or buy options are limited, such a system or change may not occur in a timely fashion. In today's world, missing this opportunity can be costly in many ways.

The material presented here is the result of many years of firsthand experience. It is hoped that those reading it will find it both of interest and of value.

RICHARD A. KAUMEYER, JR.
CANOGA PARK, CALIFORNIA

CONTENTS

1
STEPS IN DEVELOPING
A PERSONNEL SYSTEM

It is only in recent years that concern has been focused on personnel. Previously, this was considered an "overhead" or "burden" area. The function was often delegated to someone as an additional duty to supervise or manage. In small firms, a secretary was given the assignment of "handling personnel."

This was brought out in classrooms of major business and management schools. As recently as fifteen years ago, the author was attending a seminar by one of the leading consultants/lecturers in the area of management theory, who went through an elaborate evolutionary chart showing the hierarchy of living things, with humans at the top and amoebas and lesser forms at the bottom.

The drawing of this chart took place over a rather lengthy period of time. It may have been for effect, or to use up the time to make the participants feel they were getting their money's worth. If it *was* for effect, the timing was perfect. Everyone's attention was riveted on the board. What did a chart on evolution have to do with management theory? Was there some new or vital hypothesis about to be established? Were the participants attending the wrong seminar? These and many other questions and concerns were running through the minds of those present.

Finally, after what seemed to be an inordinate length of time, the lecturer turned and faced the group. He stated that he had put this chart on the board so that we could actually understand where personnel fit into the scheme of things in the organization. The evolutionary chart, with human life at the top, was to serve as the basis for an analogy.

Human life represented the senior management level in the organization. As you went down the chart, the various other corporate or organizational functions were depicted. It was only as he neared the bottom that he paused and said something to the effect of, "Here is where we find personnel—down with the worms, crawling insects, and lower forms of life." Everyone got the message loud and clear.

It is doubtful that the same analogy would go over now. Today, someone making this analogy would be challenged by a similar audience—possibly not by everyone, but certainly by a few people. There would no longer be the total agreement that once existed regarding the low esteem and value of personnel.

Times have changed, and with it, certain organizational functions have assumed new postures. It is not uncommon to find the head of personnel reporting to the president or chief executive officer. No longer is the position treated as a "roll through" slot in most major organizations. The position has become complex, and to be properly administered, a rather detailed and technical body of knowledge is required.

The name personnel seems to be changing as well. More frequently, we hear the term "human resource management" or some derivative thereof applied. This attempt to rename the function is also indicative of the new or different way it is viewed.

The problem with this renaming is the resulting confusion and misunderstanding that always accompanies such an act. Most people have some idea of what "personnel" does or is supposed to do, but few can deal with the new "human resource management" term. It probably took many years for the word "personnel" to become commonplace, and will take a similar number to absorb the new derivative(s).

The growth in importance of "human resources" is depicted in Fig. 1-1. Originally a basic recordkeeping system for an organization, the human resource function was given a certain amount of power and prestige by union activity, since the personnel group was the one most frequently negotiated with by the unions, and the group that provided various levels of management with contract interpretations.

Though personnel and unions are adversary by definition, it was the existence of unions that gave true initial recognition to the personnel function—specifically to the employee/labor relations aspect (see the top half of Fig. 1-2). In some firms, labor relations has been split off

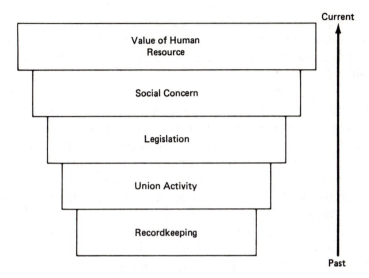

Fig. 1-1. Value of human resource (personnel) function.

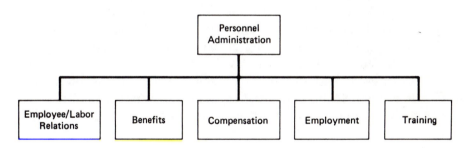

Traditional personnel function.

Personnel function (employee/labor relations separate).

Fig. 1-2.

into a separate entity (see the lower half of Fig. 1-2). There is no "rule of thumb" on this and, as in many organizations' decisions, there is a tendency to organize around the strengths of the individuals involved.

In the past, personnel has had a stronger role in organizations in which a union exists, as opposed to those organizations that are non-union. The ability of an existing union to stop production, and even to close the plant, has had a direct bearing on the position/reporting relationship of the personnel department. It has not been uncommon for the head of personnel to report at a much higher level where a strong union exists than would his or her counterpart in a non-union environment.

More frequently, legislation in areas such as affirmative action, retirement, and confidentiality has added new dimension to the personnel function. The legal implications have been significant in increasing personnel's importance. The threat of lawsuits, violations of the law, bad publicity, fines, etc., has given the personnel function the role of internal advisor on selected legal points. In many cases, personnel people are the ones who must decide when to call for internal or external legal assistance. There is an ever-increasing body of personnel-related laws impacting in many areas. A chapter will be devoted to recent and significant laws.

Another event has also recently brought personnel to the forefront. This is referred to here as social concern, and is not limited to the affirmative action activity involving women and minorities. There is a much broader sense of corporate responsibility toward employees than has previously existed.

Management no longer has the latitude they once possessed to fire an individual, nor even to lay them off in an economic downturn. There is a growing feeling, at least in the United States, that people are entitled to their jobs. Some have said that this right to a job closely parallels guarantees and rights similar to "property rights." There is an implied contract binding the employer on making a hiring decision not to release the employee without very substantial justification.

This is not to say that, in a major economic downturn, layoffs do not or will not occur. However, in minor recessions, firms are expected to maintain their workforce, if at all possible, and handle any

Fig. 1-3. A direct relationship between the price (cost) of labor and the effort to value the human resource.

slack by attrition. This is particularly true of larger organizations. Those not adhering to this are subject to a number of social sanctions, including bad press and recruiting problems when times get better.

This has caused many firms to more closely look at the hiring commitment as they would any other "contract." There is more of a tendency to screen and select more carefully. When release is inevitable, due to economic conditions, we are seeing the tendency to use outplacement firms to assist in finding new positions, loans of staff to competitors, severance pay packages, etc.

This relates directly to a change in the philosophy of the user groups (those who employ people). Greater effort is being made to place a value on the human resources. Cheap labor is almost a thing of the past and, in a labor-intensive operation, it is critical to optimize efficiency (see Fig. 1-3).

DEFINITION OF A PERSONNEL SYSTEM

Immediately, when the term "system" is used, many (if not most) people think of a computer. This is unfortunate, for several reasons. First, the concept that we have to have a computer limits our scope. A large percentage of the functions in the personnel area has been manual in nature, and probably a large number will continue to be manual in the future. Second, the concept of a computer or the possible use of one intimidates a lot of people. All of a sudden, the image conjured up is of something very complex requiring detailed technical knowledge.

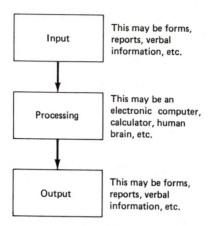

Fig. 1-4. Classical system.

The classical definition of a system implies certain steps—normally input, processing, and output (see Fig. 1-4). The processing portion may or may not be an electronic computer. However, the processing portion does not have to be a computer. It is frequently any number of things, including a calculator, and possibly no more electronic than the human brain. Looking at it this way, the "system concept" becomes more realistic and non-threatening.

Many people, both within personnel and without, are dealing with systems every day, but do not recognize them as such. The question then arises as to why we want to recognize them as such. The reason may lie in the logical sequence implied—input, processing, and output. With this understanding, we can better and more efficiently approach the work area. Once an identification of the specific system with a problem or concern has been made, we can again approach the review in a logical manner. Is the trouble in the input, processing, or output portion? A logical approach will produce the best results in problem solving.

BENEFITS TO THE ORGANIZATION

The question is asked immediately: "Why do we need an overall personnel system?" One answer, but certainly not the only answer, was just developed in our definition. A personnel system provides the basis for logically solving problems. This has to be an item of significant importance, due to the higher value an effective organization must place on problem solving.

Another important item is the "definition" a personnel system provides the organization. When this truly exists, management has a clearer picture of which functions are performed in the personnel department, and by whom these functions are performed. This has potential for improving management's ability to better assign the functions to be performed and to improve overall performance.

We are also able to identify those functions or activities that aren't being performed that should be. Frequently, it is erroneously assumed that all personnel functions in a personnel department are being performed that are generic to the activity. It is probably no real surprise that this is not the case. If it were, there would not be the large number of personnel functions "bootlegged" or performed outside of their respective areas. This is symptomatic that provisions for certain functions have not been adequately made, and the user groups have been forced to look to other resources.

This negative benefit (finding functions or activities that have been overlooked) is not often recognized. However, its value can be very significant. By its very nature, the user (customer) has either had to do without this service or develop alternate sources. The chances of the function or activity being performed by an inexperienced person are greater. Hence, the negative aspect is compounded.

Another item that a developed personnel system provides is the basis to further redesign and develop the activity. With a defined system in place, there is a starting point for future systems development. In very simple terms, it provides the foundation and framework to build and expand as our needs dictate. If the system has not been identified and defined, we have to do so before making any changes or run the risk of adding to the existing confusion. You will frequently note this problem in personnel departments that must spend all of their time on unanticipated "emergency crash projects," or work-related "fire drills." This is indicative of never-defined systems or of adding to or changing a system that has not been properly identified or defined.

It is possible to go on for several pages to list all the potential benefits that can be derived from possessing an up-to-date personnel system. However, this might be an appropriate place to stop, with one final word—visibility. In reviewing the benefits listed and imagining the long list that could result if we continued in this manner, we come up with the continuous thread or recurring concept of visibility. Knowing what is going on with the various functions in a department has value. An updated and defined system provides this visibility.

PHASES OF DEVELOPING THE PERSONNEL SYSTEM

It seems logical, if we are going to develop a personnel system, that we take a systematic approach in doing this. There are various combinations of ways of going about this. One way, and a rather effective way, is shown in Fig. 1-5. It takes us through four stages of an overview, system specification, programming or technical specification, and testing and implementation.

This term "initial phases" is important. It is not meant to imply that these are all the phases in systems design. This approach is taken to aid in answering the question that is frequently posed: "Where does one start?" It is felt that the starting point has too often been

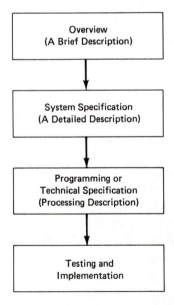

Fig. 1-5. Initial phases in designing a personnel system.

cloaked in technical jargon and needs to be unmasked and fully identified.

An overview is nothing magical or mysterious. It should be a brief definition of what management expects the system to do. The length will vary according to the size and number of functions performed in the specific personnel department, as well as the complexity of the processing unit(s) involved. These can range from one to two pages in a small manual system to thirty or forty pages in a large computer-based system.

This aspect, though important, is frequently overlooked. This is the definition and agreement phase. Here is where we define what is going to go into the system and, by exclusion, what is not going into it, and whether the system will be automated or manual. This document should be prepared in layman's terms and define in broad parameters how the system will work.

The overview, though not specific in detail, serves a very important purpose. It is in writing, and it states in general terms what the system is going to do. This gives those with any real concerns or expectations an opportunity to voice them. There is an old, but accurate saying: "If you want to find out who the experts are, just put something in writing." Truer words were never spoken! The system overview tends to smoke out the silent majority. It tends to do this at the beginning of the effort, while there is still the opportunity for modification, rather than after completion, when things are locked into place.

The overview should solicit input from all of those who might be involved. Figure 1-6 depicts the wide variety of areas (not all-inclusive) with which we might want to coordinate the written overview. It is important to have the initial document reviewed by anyone who would have an interest in doing so. We particularly want to have it reviewed by personnel management, personnel non-management, general management, and other user groups that don't fall into the first categories.

Some may take exception to having those outside of management circles involved in the review process. However, it is frequently the non-management portion of the team that must work with and depend on the system to perform daily tasks. Management frequently is aware of the system only as a place to go to get general questions

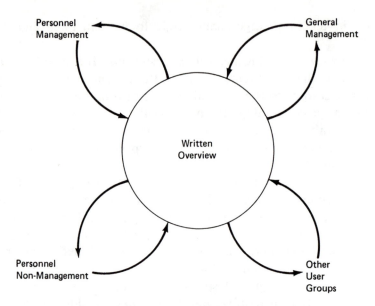

Personnel
Management

General
Management

Written
Overview

Personnel
Non-Management

Other
User
Groups

Fig. 1-6. Coordination possibilities of written overview.

answered, or when it fails to work properly. The non-management group that works with the system on a daily basis has a more intimate grasp of the details of the specific day-to-day operation. Ultimately, this is what we want to run smoothly; hence, it is an area not to be overlooked.

A system specification is the next step after agreement on the overview. This is more detailed and can run from several pages to book-length, or even into multiple volumes (in a multinational organization). Here is where the details on how the system is to run should be reduced to writing. This is the day-to-day or hour-by-hour description of the system.

Too frequently, the mistakes are made trying to prepare this part based on the existing system, plus whatever additional enhancements are desired. It is analogous to building a room addition on an existing house. This is acceptable if you are satisfied with the existing house. However, if the intent is to build a brand new house, a room addition on an old structure with which you are completely dissatisfied is worthless.

The same is true with a system. We too often just build onto an existing mess. What we wind up with is a mess with an add-on, which is hardly the intent. We should be following the guidelines of the overview in doing our system specification. However, these guidelines tend to be, by design, broad and general. It is very easy to start preparing the system specification by focusing on where we are now, and not on where we want to go.

The system specification phase is a time of research, a time to target what is needed. You can usually identify a system specification that is being done improperly. The analysts are focusing on the existing reports and on what needs to be added. In essence, they are building on the "existing mess." Unfortunately, too many personnel systems are designed this way.

The analysts should be focusing on what data elements are needed. We really don't care what reports are needed in the initial phase. This should come much later, or almost at the end of the initial study. The data elements and their definition should be the first step.

Questions focusing on the need for employee number, social security number, starting date of employment, beginning salary, current salary, etc., should be the first step. Then, these data elements must be defined so that concurrence exists by everyone on the meaning. Figure 1-7 depicts the order of importance.

Only at the end or near the end of the system specification should the analysts work with the organization on the design of the reports.

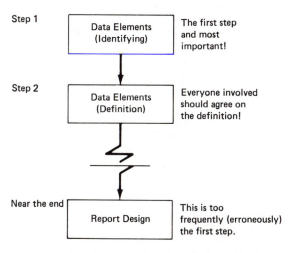

Fig. 1-7. Order of importance: System specification.

Here we fully utilize the data elements and definition. The design of the reports can be both freer and more expanded, since we are no longer bound by past constraints. Those reports developed at this stage meet the needs of the organization. They frequently have no resemblance to the existing reports. In this way, a truly new system has been developed, one that is in line with the requirements of those involved.

When the system has been defined, another logical step is to put it into some form of a processing description. For want of a better term, it is referred to here as the "programming (or technical) specification." Too often, the term "programming" immediately locks out any system but a computer-based one.

Here this is not the case, and a manual personnel system is just as viable an option. If we were to do a survey, the findings would indicate a preponderance of manual systems. Even in large organizations in which computer usage has proliferated, manual portions of the system continue to be numerous and active. A *fact,* which should be underlined, is that most systems start out in some manual form and only after having proven themselves are they converted to a computer.

Rather than a programming specification, the term "technical specification" may be more appropriate. It immediately includes both manual and machine approaches. It also implies the "technical" nature of this specification. For it is here that the steps in the processing portion of the activity are defined in detail. For a computer-based operation, it will be the steps and explanation needed for the programmer to code the system into computer language. In a manual system, it will be the related processing instructions necessary to performing the function (e.g., detailed definition of data evaluation or arithmetic calculations).

The final step indicated here would be the testing or implementation phase. In a computer system the coding or programming would also be accomplished. Some may feel the series of steps indicated is too abbreviated. It must be remembered that what we are trying to achieve at this point is a basic definition. A macro or overall view is being established to set the basic framework. The testing or implementation phase puts a cap on this overview.

The testing or implementation phase is important. If approached and used properly, a tremendous value to the system can be achieved.

On the other hand, if done improperly, a serious work impediment, if not a total disaster, may occur.

Too often, a cavalier approach is taken regarding testing and final implementation. This is natural, since it seems that the most technical and detailed work has been accomplished by the time we reach this phase. It may, however, be a bit like canning: If you don't put the lid on properly, everything spoils and all that went before is lost.

Problems tend to arise, particularly where the system is replacing one that is already in place. An almost certain formula for trouble is to turn off one system and rely totally on the new system before properly testing and checking it. Any new system, regardless of how well designed, has problems that need to be identified and corrected. Proper time must be allocated to achieve this.

The easiest way may be to run both systems (the old and the new) at the same time. This is frequently referred to as parallel testing. With this method, if the new system fails, the information data, etc., from the old system is there as a back-up. The longer this can be continued, the more problems that can be resolved without the loss to the operating aspect of the operation. Usually, the length of time of a parallel test is restricted by the cost of running and maintaining two separate systems.

OBTAINING MANAGEMENT SUPPORT

No system is going to get off the ground unless it has the blessing of key managers. These are the people who may not only use the system, but must allocate the funds, time, and other resources necessary for its success. The larger the magnitude of the personnel system, the more important this area of support.

The higher the level of support for the system, the greater the chance for its success and implementation. Too often, system support is sought laterally or among peer groups. This type of support can be of value. It is, however, dwarfed when the support comes from the office of the president or chairman of the board.

Frequently, those proposing a personnel system don't think of seeking this level of support. But just look at the cost of human resources today. "Cheap labor" is almost nonexistent in developed countries and is quickly going the way of the dinosaur in underdeveloped countries.   There are few places on this globe where the cost of labor is not a critical decision-making factor.   Hence, every chief executive officer (at least those who plan on continuing in that position) is concerned about the use of human resources. This use and effective management is the target of the personnel system.

The art of presenting any proposal at this level is knowing the area of interest.   For example, a peer group presentation to middle management will usually focus on how it will help get the daily job done—or what new and more sophisticated information will be available. The chief executive, although interested in this data, will want to focus on concerns related to the health of the overall organization. These include items such as: What is the cost? What is the return on the dollar invested? How soon will the return occur? Every decision at this level must focus on how it impacts on the "earnings per share" or a related bottom line measure.

Those introducing new systems may forget that their presentations must vary with the audience involved. Once this is recognized, the task becomes easier. The information is there; it is a matter of knowing which parts are available for which audiences.

OBTAINING EMPLOYEE SUPPORT

The larger the personnel system, the more important obtaining employee support can be. No system survives in a vacuum, and no system can survive without support. There are a number of reasons for obtaining employee support in the initial phases.

More and more systems that maintain information on employees—which a personnel system generally does—are open for inspection to those on whom the information is kept. Those who are involved in the development of such a system tend to be more supportive later, and sensitive areas of concern can be identified before they become major problems.

Another important factor is that it is usually the employee who must work with the system on a daily basis. It is the employee who must perform that input/output—not management. We frequently overlook this very important fact when designing the system. The desires of management are built in, but what about the people who must live with the system and make it work?

In addition, if only management is consulted about the system design, we miss a truly valuable resource. Those who work with a system on a daily basis may know only a portion of it—but they know this portion in intimate detail. This is the type of information that can aid in system design. Here is a resource that can be tapped and produce information vital to smooth day-to-day operation.

How does one go about tapping it? The important thing is to remember that non-management employees may require a different approach as well as significantly more time for explanation. But the benefit derived is usually worth the effort.

Management frequently has "the big picture." Consequently, circulating written material on the system with a short follow-up individual meeting may suffice. However, these same techniques may not work with individual non-management people, since they don't have the broader vision. They have only detailed knowledge of selected portions. Here we may opt for individual one-on-one interviews or small group reviews.

There is additional time and personal contact needed to provide the missing overview that this resource does not have. It cannot be assumed that employees know the new system will be beneficial. Time and individual attention must be given to explain the new system and the relationship of the employee's portion. This preliminary information is needed so that the employee can better describe the changes to his/her portion that would benefit the entire package.

2
MANUAL SYSTEMS

A personnel system does not have to be computer based! This was stressed earlier, but the message, even with multiple repetitions, does not seem to get through to many people. The term "system" conjures up an expensive computer complex that is highly technical, with its lights winking and blinking. Along with this comes the vision of high-priced technical specialists to operate the sophisticated equipment.

In some cases, this is true—particularly in large firms. However, many total systems in smaller firms are better left in a manual state. Also, selected portions of systems in large firms are, and will continue to be, manual, for a variety of reasons. In some cases, security of information dictates this (e.g., profit-sharing plans of selected senior executives). New systems in a research and development (R & D) phase may not be defined enough to automate, and such systems would by necessity be manual.

CRITERIA FOR A MANUAL SYSTEM

There are no hard and fast rules as to when to have a manual person-nel system and when to automate. However, there are some guide-lines that we can use. One criterion is shown in Fig. 2-1. This is the size criterion.

Firms that are smaller in staff size may find that a manual system will meet their needs. On the average, because exceptions can be cited, a firm tends to remain in a manual state until the population reaches eight to twelve hundred employees. It is generally at this number that the benefits of automating become more pronounced.

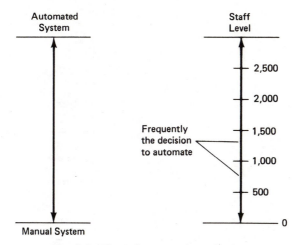

Fig. 2-1. Manual system size criterion.

(This target number drops as the cost of automation decreases.) Growth can slip up rather fast on organization. The leap of four or five hundred people may occur almost overnight, and often necessitates a too-rapid conversion from a manual to an automated system.

This is intertwined with the strategic planning of the organization. The more the changes to the size of the organization have been planned and communicated, the less the chance of a problem arising that would catch those involved off-guard. However, strategic planning in organizations of all sizes is too often viewed as a luxury, rather than the necessity that it is. Thus, we find many managers involved in the day-to-day activity of spending their time with emergencies (frequently called "fire fighting") instead of doing the job of managing for which they are being paid.

One reason a concrete or exact number of people can't be given in Fig. 2-1 is that the design of the existing manual system is a factor. The better the manual system is in design, the longer and more durable it will be as the staff population increases. A well-designed system can more easily handle increased volume. This, in turn, will postpone the need to automate for a greater length of time.

Another criterion for when to automate is shown in Fig. 2-2. This is referred to as the "Human Resource Information Complexity." In common language, this is the data or information required or main-

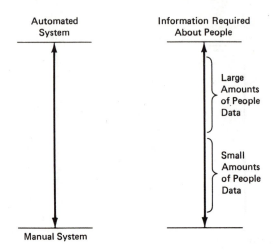

Fig. 2-2. Manual system human resource information complexity.

tained on the people in a given organization. As the amount of data per individual increases, the more a move toward automation is likely to occur.

The sources creating this increase in human resource data may be external in origin. Government requirements can be a major external factor. Union contracts may require specific information (e.g., union dues deductions, bargaining unit code, etc.) to be maintained. Normally, these external factors add to the amount of information maintained. However, there have been recent trends to limit or restrict information of a personal nature.

The overall tendency of outside or external factors has been to provoke continual increase in people-related data.

An equally large impact is from the internal side. This is the data that management wants to collect on people. Historically, this was limited to basic payroll information. Now we find data requirements from basic application information extending to the capture of various skill identifiers.

The world is becoming more complex as technology broadens and develops new horizons. This complexity is extended into the jobs that support these changes. Consequently, the people performing the functions must have appropriate backgrounds to get the work done. Management, in turn, is charged with the responsibility of "staffing."

The more and better information available, the easier and more effective management can be in performing the staffing function.

Another criterion that may determine whether a system will be manual or automated is whether the personnel system is centralized or decentralized. Decentralization can cut down on the volume of records that have to be handled to answer specific personnel questions. The data manipulation is spread over a greater number of individuals.

As with any decision, cost is a significant factor. Historically, personnel was low on the totempole, even in large organizations, to have the opportunity to automate. For years, the data processing resource was scarce and rationed to line organizations, rather than to staff. While it has proliferated, cost is still a significant factor.

Initially, the costs of automating any system were very high. Advances in technology, combined with greater supply of services and increased competition, continues to bring the cost down. Package systems that can operate in multiple organizations with limited modifications also have added to the reduction. The ability to lease time through a terminal, rather than buying a computer, has put the computer in the reach of almost anyone, without having to commit to a major capital outlay.

One of the drawbacks to most existing automated systems is the cost in the level of staff required to operate such a system. In many cases, we have to have a staff of higher technical level to operate an automated system. Labor is no longer an inexpensive commodity— particularly highly skilled technical labor.

Eventually, technology will conquer at least a portion of the staff problem. We will, at some point in the near future, be able to communicate with the computer by voice the same way as we would with an individual. Direct voice communication has been looming on the horizon for years, and it is actually being used operationally in some instances.

When this becomes universal, a significant operation breakthrough will have arrived. The need for a typewriter terminal and special languages to be learned will be gone. The staff member requiring specific answers, data manipulation, special reports, and so on will be able to ask the device for it in everyday conversational language. The device will respond with the necessary information in a vocal or printed conversational mode. This will allow both parties to explore and clarify what is wanted without the complicated translator steps.

When the costs of such devices are in the range of salaries of clerks who would do the same work, we have a viable alternative. Figure 2-3 depicts this transition. The two items that could change a manual decision are (1) a rapid or unexpected increase in the cost of a firm's labor and (2) a significant decrease in the cost of automation. When either or both occurs, we will select the machine option.

LOCATING MANUAL SYSTEMS

Those who feel their organizations fit in the category requiring a manual system may want to improve their existing systems. Some may be in a position of starting a completely new system. In either case, they are normally trying to identify information sources. Where do they go to review manual systems in order to identify those in existence that best fit their requirements?

One of the first sources to explore is other organizations of a similar size in related fields of endeavor. Most organizations (even competitors) are willing to share and exchange personnel systems infor-

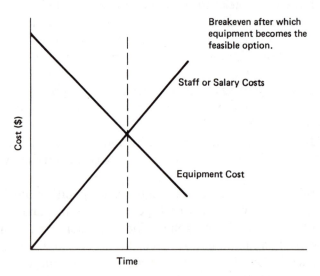

Fig. 2-3. Equipment versus staff or salary costs.

mation. People in the personnel field generally have a camaraderie that facilitates this type of exchange.

This is a major resource that frequently remains untapped. Most people say they are uncomfortable because they don't know anyone to call. An excellent starting point is through a mutual acquaintance from a professional organization, a local university, or another firm. It is usually easier for those that are uncomfortable making these calls to at least be able to mention someone who referred them.

Another source is a consultant. These can be identified by the same sources that were suggested previously—professional organizations, local universities, or acquaintances in other firms. One of the key factors to look for is the consultant's prior experience with manual systems.

There are a number of things an outside consultant brings to the situation. Included among these (but not limited to them) would be experience with similar situations, speed in implementation, and third party creditability. Consultants are thought to be too expensive and out of reach, but before this assumption is made, it is wise to obtain bids and do a cost comparison. Often, you will find that the cost of an outside consultant is actually less than the cost of using internal resources—particularly when you take into account the learning time the internal resources need to come up to speed.

KNOWING WHEN IT IS TIME TO CONVERT

As was discussed earlier, systems do change. There are occasions when manual systems evolve into automated systems. But, although less heralded, there are times when the reverse is true. Regardless, the important factor is to know when change is truly called for and when no action should be taken.

The same criteria apply that were noted under the heading *Criteria for a Manual System.* Size is most often the determining factor. Generally, when an organization reaches a total number of around eight hundred, manual systems become cumbersome. Management and others can no longer obtain flexible human resource information in a timely manner.

It is usually at this point that people, because of their numbers, play a significant part in the management decision-making process.

An increase in the cost of any of the cost components (direct pay, benefits, etc.) for the group has substantial total dollar impact. At the same time, new information requirements are more difficult to deal with because of the numbers involved. Flexibility and response time become reduced and problems arise when management requests are continually denied.

As noted, the change in size frequently occurs rapidly. The transition from a situation in which the personnel system is working well to a chaotic time of trouble can occur in a short time. However, if the growth is slow and steady without any large spurts, the system just decays over time with a slowly increasing rate of dissatisfaction.

Size, of course, is not the only factor. Information complexity, decentralization, and cost of equipment, labor, etc. can have a major impact on the decision to automate. These are all criteria to be weighed along with size.

Again, the importance of the strategic planning system in any organization must be stressed. We need to know if we are going to expand or contract, as well as the speed at which this might occur. The structure is not totally predictable, but alternate scenarios can be established. If activity is going to increase by 10% over the next year, we might want to establish a different set of alternatives than if it goes to 25%, and yet a different set should it go to 50%. Laying out these alternatives and the related actions allows us to define the alternate actions we may need to take.

Planning gives us options. It allows an organization to take the actions that are in its best interest, rather than to be in a defensive mode and react to unanticipated events. When we react in this way, we are operating from a point of weakness. However, when we act from a plan, events can be more frequently shaped to allow opportunities to develop.

People too often feel that strategic planning is useless, since they may not be able to fully implement the original plan. In essence, they will have to deviate as other events or activities cause them to modify their original position. This, in fact, is the heart of strategic planning. With a plan, we have a focus of reference, or a point from which to deviate. This deviation allows us to obtain the most optimal goals and achievements.

The often overlooked (or not mentioned) option in conversion, which has been alluded to here, is the reverse of going from an automated to a manual system. This can, and does, happen. Too many people think of an automated system as a status symbol. Going from automation to a manual system is erroneously thought of as being analogous to going from a jet plane to a wagon train.

Both manual and automated systems have their value. Organizational decisions should be based on facts and logic rather than on emotion. Since people are involved in making these decisions, emotions will nevertheless enter into them, but it is hoped that facts and logic will prevail in the decision-making process.

The decision to switch to a manual system is based on the reverse of the criteria previously noted. Again, size becomes a major factor, along with the others that have been noted. Organizational growth is generally an expectation, while reduction may be a temporary phenomenon. Length of time of the reduction may become another significant factor in the decision. If the time is considered to be of short duration and/or possibly cyclical, the decision to abandon the automated system may be modified accordingly. This is depicted in Fig. 2-4. This figure assumes that only organization size within a certain

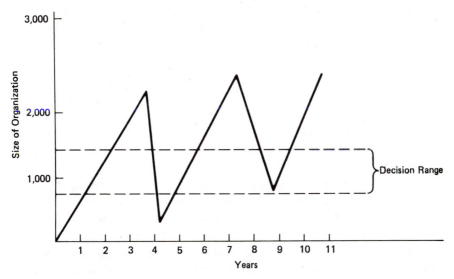

Fig. 2-4. Manual/automated decision process. (Fluctuation in one of the major criteria, such as population, complicates the decision.)

range has a major decision-making impact. Realistically, this is but one factor and the "decision range" can, and will, vary substantially based on input of other criteria, such as information complexity, centralization/decentralization, and cost of equipment, labor, etc.

AVOIDING DISRUPTION IN WORK FLOW

Implementing any new system, whether from manual to automated or the reverse, can have disruptive effects. Most organizations can't just stop what they are doing to implement the new system. A transition plan must be developed to assure that existing output continues as the transition is implemented.

We discussed the consideration of running the systems in parallel. If an older system is in operation, it should be continued for as long as possible until the new one has been thoroughly checked out. This, of course, is limited by the costs of doing this, which are based on such factors as staff, equipment, and time, etc.

Another, and too frequently overlooked, way of avoiding disruption is involvement of the people affected. Management spends large portions of time and effort focusing on the technical/mechanical aspects of the system. In the final analysis, systems are either made or broken by the human element involved. If those who must operate and use the system daily don't want the system to work, you can bet that it is not going to work!

The quickest way to alienate people is not to involve them in the initial decision-making process. The best way to assure failure is to keep the system quiet and secretive, and spring it on those who must deal with it just as you are ready to start using it. We all resist change and the unknown. If the new system is viewed as something new and as somebody else's idea, it will be resisted.

To avoid these kinds of problems, and to assure smooth (or at least a smoother) implementation, involve people in the conceptual phase. And we don't want to be too selective about whom we involve. If there is a question as to whether someone will or will not work with the system, he or she should be included. Rank should not be a factor. High or low on the organization totempole, all who might have use, contact, etc., should be contacted early. Their input/suggestions should be solicited at the same time that they are made aware of the future potential change.

There is usually substantial lead time from conceptualization to implementation of any system. Involving people early allows us to take advantage of this time factor. In fact, the time factor helps to assure the smooth implementation we are seeking. Those who are informed up front have a chance to "mentally digest" the change. Ultimately, as with any change, it becomes the norm rather than something brand new. The future becomes the present.

Additionally, soliciting input/suggestions gives a sense of ownership. The system is not as threatening when one is part of the decision-making process. It is then not "the system," but "our system" that makes a significant difference in the level of effort to assure success. Also, the input from those who must work with the system can be invaluable. Different visibility exists at various levels in the organization. To work properly, a system must meet the needs of everyone who uses it. This is true in both manual and automated systems.

3
COMPUTER SYSTEMS

The sequel to a manual system, of course, is an automated or computer system. In actuality, there are few systems that are completely manual in every sense, or that are completely automated. Most systems that are referred to as manual have some source material, either internal or external to the organization, that is processed via automated means. By the same token, most organizations that refer to themselves as having an automated personnel system rely heavily on multiple manual support systems in various phases of their operation.

The move toward automation generally evolves over a period of time. Almost every system that is automated was, at one time or another, manual. Take a few minutes and think about an organization you are familiar with that has an "automated" personnel system. Chances are very good that several major portions of the operation are not automated. Also, chances are excellent that any new enhancement to the system will go through a research and development (R & D) phase that will be manual. A large percentage of "pilot" testing is frequently kept in the manual phase. It costs less and can be modified with more ease. Of course, as costs go down, more of these R & D systems can be tested in an automated environment, if applicable.

TYPES OF COMPUTER SYSTEMS AVAILABLE

Established computerized personnel systems usually have sources identified for minor revision and even major system development. There is a unique question that comes up with organizations starting to convert to a computerized personnel system: "Where does one go to find a computerized personnel system?"

There are really two major options available. The first is to design the system internally, or to "make it." The second is to "buy" the system. Buying a system constitutes either finding a package system that meets your needs and purchasing it, or having someone outside your organization modify an existing one or design one to fit your needs.

Many firms immediately decide they will design (or make) their own system, the concern being that outside help (or buying) will be too expensive. Here a major problem results (this is depicted in Fig. 3-1). Automatically, the decision to purchase is rejected, and the decision to make a system is accepted. This would be fine if the internal resources existed to design such a personnel system. Too often, the organization is too small to support the talent on its own, and the

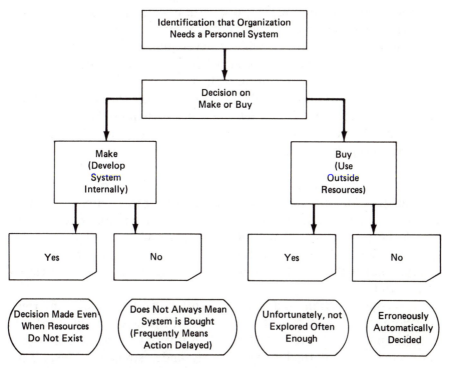

Fig. 3-1. Problems involved in the decision to make or buy a system.

organization also comes to the realization of its need for such a system when the existing manual system starts to fail. The situation has by then gone into a crisis mode.

Building a system not only takes the talent that is sometimes not present, it takes time as well. If the existing system is not meeting the organization's needs, time has already run out! Usually, panic sets in and task forces and senior management review committees are established to assure speedy and correct system implementation. This just makes the bad situation worse. What results parallels a managerial or organizational equivalent of the Keystone Cops! The blind end up leading the blind. Review committees just buy time and accomplish nothing except to formalize saying "no." It is unfortunate, but it frequently takes years for this to be recognized—and some organizations never admit this has been, or is, happening to them. The symptoms are usually the same: Everyone agrees a new personnel system is critically needed, but it *just never appears*.

There are often impressive presentations—graphs, charts, etc.—circulated. Brochures, memos, and outlines may laud how good the new system will be, but it seems like it never comes to pass. After many years, a system finally comes into being, and may very well come close to the original description. The only problem is that it is too late. The organization's needs have evolved, and the system is often partially, if not totally, obsolete. Then efforts must be undertaken to set up the mechanism to modify the system. This, if handled in the same way as the original system design, just perpetuates a vicious circle. The system stays in a never-ending circle of development and revision, never meeting the organizational requirements.

The question arises as to how to avoid having this happen. A starting point may be to honestly evaluate the existing in house resources. Does the present staff have the capability and prior experience in developing such systems? If not, and we still want to develop internally, what is the cost to hire people to bring our internal staff capability up to speed?

A second question, and one that is often overlooked with internal development, is time. How much time will it take our own staff to design and develop such a system? This is very hard to quantify, and projections tend normally to be grossly underestimated. The ability to accurately produce estimates seems to be a function of prior experience working on personnel systems. The larger the number of systems the estimator had been involved with, the closer the estimate usually comes to reality.

One thing to remember is that we have a viable option to developing the system internally: We can "buy" the system. There are several alternatives in the external purchase or buy decision. The entire system can be purchased, or technical guidance (consultants) can be brought in to direct the internal resources. Additionally, there are all the combinations and permutations of these two options.

Possibly the most important time item is recognition that there are alternatives and not just automatically writing off outside resources as too costly without making a comparison. Looking at the cost of the buy decision can be misleading. Usually, we are looking at the purchase price or per diem rate of the vendor or consultant! There are other factors involved that are just as important.

One of these is the time involved. The cost in dollars may be less if development is internal, but is anything saved if it takes three, four, or five years to have the system operating? Very few internally developed personnel systems are up and running within a few months. There is no value if, by the time a system is in place, it is obsolete. External sources may be able to have the system up and running in a matter of weeks or a few months.

Another consideration of importance is whether the system fits the organization. Every organization has its own unique personality, just as it has its own structure. The personnel system must be tailored to fit this or it will be rejected by its users. The internally developed or made system generally does this. The system bought may or may not be tailored to incorporate the organization's terms and steps in operating. This is one of the points to be spelled out in the contract if we decide to go to an external source.

The analysis sheet in Fig. 3-2 depicts this. It also stresses that consideration should be given to alternate ways of obtaining a personnel system. Different factors are shown and will have varying values to different organizations. It is hoped that it will serve as a guide and a prod to look at more than one possibility.

COMBINING MANUAL AND MACHINE SYSTEMS

As was noted, very few systems are totally manual. Most systems rely on some input either internally or externally (someone else's sys-

	Factors		
	Initial $ Cost	Time to Deliver	Fits the Organization
Develop Internally			
Purchase the Entire System			
Purchase Consulting in System Development			

Fig. 3-2. Make or buy analysis sheet.

tem) that is automated. An example might be employee paychecks that are manually processed and may be cancelled and returned via an automated banking system.

On the other side of the coin, very few systems are totally automated. In even the most sophisticated system, selected portions are processed manually for varying reasons. Included in these are a wide range of requirements such as special security for high-level executives, cost effectiveness, and R & D (detailed previously).

The point to be emphasized is that few systems are totally in one category or the other. There are occasions where this is not recognized and problems result. This seems to occur most frequently with automated systems. The philosophy develops that everything must be automated. Some things may not be tested sufficiently to automate or can't be justified for such treatment in dollars-and-cents terms.

Automating for the sake of automating can be counterproductive. The decision should always be based on the most effective media. Automation is not necessarily the best and most modern way to handle a specific function, nor is operating in a manual mode necessarily negative. The end goal is to perform the function in the most efficient and effective manner possible.

SELECTING A COMPUTER SYSTEM

There are similarities in the decision process used to determine where information exists between a manual and automated system. In both cases, we want to start by avoiding "reinventing the wheel." We want to find out what other organizations in similar or related types of activities have done or are planning to do. This information is available through a number of sources including personal contacts, professional organizations, and local universities.

The decision must be resolved as to whether we are going to make or buy. If the decision is to make, the existing resources must be evaluated and expanded as required. Then the group should be directed to analyze what others are doing in the personnel systems area under study. This provides management, both general and technical, with a benchmark to determine what positive things others are using that they wish to incorporate in their system, and which new items must be developed.

If the decision is to buy, a similar activity must take place. More than a single system or package must be reviewed. Sufficient vendors should be reviewed to provide a good selection. There are now enough vendors present in the area of automated personnel systems to provide options. This is an important process for an organization, since an automated system often commits substantial funds. Also, by its very nature, it may be difficult to easily reverse, change, or modify when it is in place.

Having identified those vendors who might have potential, we should ask them to submit preliminary proposals. After reviewing and identifying the most promising, we want to add or include any additional specifications or modifications appropriate for our organization. With these included, we would ask the three or four most promising vendors for a revised proposal/bid. This would give us an excellent basis for making the final decision.

Depending on our in-house expertise to survey the market, arrange proposals, etc., one may wish to hire a consultant who has some expertise in this field to assist. This selection should be someone who, as an independent, is not connected with any of the vendors involved. This precludes a conflict of interest situation. Such a knowledgeable third party can be valuable in the various analysis involved in this process.

DETERMINING MANAGEMENT'S NEEDS

Figure 3-3 depicts a few of the multiple organizational require-ments that control the system design. The four shown here are sig-nificant, but not inclusive. Each organization has its own vested interest groups. Those that are the most vocal and persistent fre-quently have a major influence on how the system is designed.

Senior managers often gained a large portion of both their educa-tion and experience before computer-based systems were prevalent. There is not always the comfort level with automation that now exists with younger members who grew up with the computer as a "given." We frequently tend to delegate to others those things that we are unfamiliar or uncomfortable with. This very natural tendency can cause problems when a computer-based system is under design.

The people who are the leaders in other aspects of the organiza-tion's activities (management) may not assume this role in the design of a computer-based system. The knowledge, experience, guidance, etc., available to guide other aspects of the organization's activity, may be missing. The first step in dealing with this problem is recog-nizing the likelihood of its existence.

Special effort may be required to assure that management's needs are identified. There is not a magic technique for doing this. Possibly,

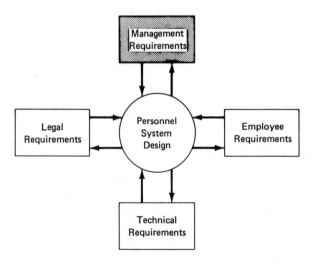

Fig. 3-3. System design controlled by multiple organizational requirements.

the most important factor is the very recognition that extra effort must be taken. More time must be spent in assuring the basic system's concepts are both presented and understood. Extra time should be spent by the analyst individually with the members of the management team. In a one-on-one discussion, there is greater freedom to identify and explain areas that are not clearly understood, as well as to gain specific management input on selected points.

DETERMINING PORTIONS TO AUTOMATE

When there is an automation decision, the psychology involved seems to lean toward automating everything. Automation is "good" and allowing portions to remain manual is "bad." This psychology must be identified and corrected early, or it will create higher costs and reduce the effectiveness of the system.

One test that should be applied when determining what parts to automate is cost savings. Figure 3-4 depicts the alternatives. Those areas that show a decided savings usually have priority. Borderline savings with future growth potential would be next in line. Even those that show no present savings but may be savings areas due to growth would be considered. It is sometimes less costly to build in

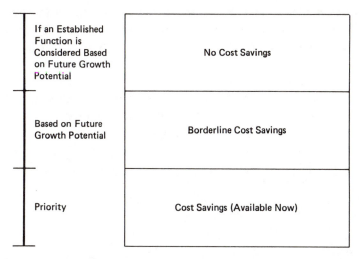

Fig. 3-4. Cost savings alternatives in determining implementation.

room for a system's expansion in the earlier phases. Anticipating future needs and providing for them can save money over a given period of time.

PORTIONS THAT DO NOT LEND THEMSELVES
TO AUTOMATION

There will also be manual portions that prove to be efficient. Again, cost is usually the major test factor. If, at a given point in time, the manual system is less costly than its computer counterpart, then one test has been met. Then if future projections indicate it will continue being cost-effective over a period of time, it does not seem wise to convert. In fact, without further justification, it could not be supported at all.

We will be designing a *personnel* system, so, by its very nature, a large percentage of the functions will deal with the human factor. Most people want the personal touch and don't want to be treated as a number. The man/machine interface has special significance. Usually, we look at it when a person has to operate a machine in performing his/her job function.

In this case, the impact of the man/machine interface is with the customer. The employee or staff member is the customer of the personnel department. Hence, we want to be sensitive to the positioning of the automated system. We want to avoid giving people the feeling they are being treated as numbers. There may be cases where automation is feasible and cost-justified in the technical sense, but not from the human relations point of view. Each function and part of the system must be examined and developed with this human relations point of view in mind, or nothing is really gained.

4
LEGAL ASPECTS OF
PERSONNEL SYSTEMS

In the United States, legal changes have had a significant impact on all aspects of personnel, not the least of which are personnel systems. These changes are frequently lamented by those involved (e.g., personnel management). However, no single item has done more to raise the status and reporting relationship of the personnel function.

Initially, it was the body of laws that sanctioned and protected union activity. This was previously noted earlier. The position of those involved in the labor relations part of personnel was established and brought to the forefront. For many years, the directors of personnel were frequently selected from the ranks of labor specialists. They were line specialists in a traditionally staff function.

Labor relations is still a significant part of the personnel function. However, it has recently been overshadowed by more current laws, which affect even broader aspects of the personnel function. These, in turn, have further enhanced the status, importance, and prestige of personnel.

NEW PERSONNEL SYSTEMS LEGALLY REQUIRED

The single most significant impact on personnel systems has probably arisen from the affirmative action area. This is the result of the laws against discrimination based on race, religion, color, sex, national origin, age, handicapped, etc.

More important than the specific statutes have been the court interpretations. These have tended to favor the individual, employee, and/

or employee groups. The organization involved has typically been found to be the responsible party. This has put both the pressure and the focus of attention on the organization.

To go over all of the laws and court decisions is not the intent either of this book or this chapter. The target is to review the general categories that affect the personnel function, and in turn impact significantly on the design considerations of a personnel system. Figure 4-1 depicts some of the major legal areas effecting personnel and related systems.

The various labor laws are the single most important factor in both the existence and development of personnel. Whether an organization has a union or not, this is true. The threat of unionization is present. We can find areas where unions are forbidden, such as in certain parts of government. Yet, even where present situations do not legally sanction them, the threat is still there. Statutes can be changed, and this is always a concern of management.

Personnel departments have not arisen because management wanted to do something nice for the employees. Personnel departments exist and have grown to protect the interests of management and the organization. The first of such actions is unionization. When a personnel department does exist, it must try to control and moderate the union's demands. The body of functions that have this task are known under the name of personnel, labor relations, employee relations, industrial relations, human resources, etc. Regardless of the name, it falls under the personnel umbrella.

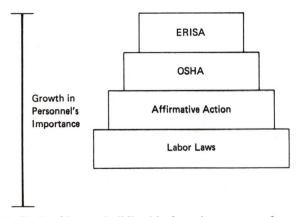

Fig. 4-1. Body of laws — building blocks to importance of personnel.

In more recent times, other laws and court interpretations have come along that have further pitted management and the employees against each other. This has given strength to the personnel department. In time of war and under threat of war, a nation strengthens its defenses and its armed forces. In the organizational arena, when dealing with employees, this defense and armed force is the personnel department. It is almost paradoxical that both the army and the personnel department owe their existence to a threat to the existing leadership.

In recent times, affirmative action has been added to unions as a concern of management. Where unions threaten management by taking money in higher salaries and fringe benefits, affirmative action does so primarily through the threats of fines and lost contracts.

Affirmative action has affected both the organization structure of the personnel department and the information it collects. Organizationally, an affirmative action function has been set up to monitor the action and handle the government-required reporting. Some data is no longer legally possible to gather, while other additional data is legally required.

For example, it would not be legal for most employers to ask an applicant his or her religion on an application form. However, employers are frequently required to provide governmental review agencies with the sex and race of people on the payroll. This has caused changes in the data collected and the personnel system used to collect it. In this instance, religion is no longer a field in the personnel data system, while sex and race must be maintained.

Because they have sanctions and punitive power, requests from government agencies cannot be ignored, negotiated, or postponed as easily as from other sources. Most organizations have to treat them as priority mandates. Consequently, the requests for information tend to increase the data elements involved in the personnel system. Each year, more information is added, with little being reduced, and the personnel system is expanded.

This growth can be seen in more current federal legislation. In 1970, the Occupational Safety and Health Act (OSHA) came into being, the prime aim being to further protect the safety and health of the worker. In many instances, this has been supplemented by state laws in the same area. Together, these statutes and related court rulings have produced added recordkeeping. This is particularly heavy in manufacturing and heavy industry, where safety and health hazards are more prevalent.

An even more recent act, titled the Employee Retirement Income Security Act (ERISA), of 1975, is still under interpretation and has had a major impact on pensions, savings plans, etc. It is very lengthy and complex, which has led to confusion and a long period of time needed to interpret various meanings. This complexity has led to its being referred to as an "Everything, Ridiculous, Insipid, Stupid, and Awful" Act by those who have to try to implement it. You will also hear it referred to as the actuaries' full employment act for the same reasons.

Most benefit groups in personnel have increased in size and scope to implement the various facets of ERISA. This is the continuing theme of all the new laws and court decisions. More work and responsibility is shifted to the personnel department. Figure 4-2 shows this change. This, in turn, has increased the power of personnel within the firm.

IMPACT ON LEGISLATION

Management reacts to the penalty or consequences of doing or not doing something. Employee dissatisfaction by itself is seldom enough

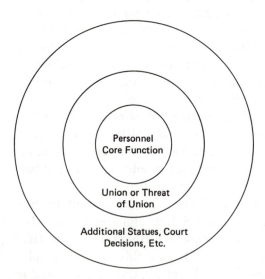

Fig. 4-2. Growth in importance of personnel.

to get management to act. However, if the organization is threatened with closure, fines, prison terms, etc., management's attention is quickly gained. Present statutes contain more sanctions of this type. This is causing not only an increase in the power of personnel due to these threats, but a shift of power from the organization to the government and legislative bodies imposing these sanctions.

Forcing an organization's management to act or react in the short term may produce the desired immediate results. It may, however, plant some very grim seeds that will be reaped in the future. Government and its related functions are not noted for exceptional managerial capabilities. The larger a body becomes, the greater its inefficiencies.

As power is shifted from the private sector to the government, the management of the private sector becomes more limited in its ability to act and react. The incentive to do so becomes negative. We ultimately may destroy the "goose that lays the golden egg" unless this trend is significantly reduced and reversed.

CHANGING PENALTIES

One of the changes observed is the move toward penalties including fines and jail sentences for failure to comply. It seems that each new law to control management is leaning in this direction. There is no question that this will get attention. However, it assumes that legislators and courts are better at running the business than are the managers.

The legislators and courts are the same ones responsible for the personal safety of the citizenry. There are few large cities in the world today where it is safe to walk the street at night. Organized terrorism exists at uncontrolled levels throughout the world. It is hard to envision that the same people who allow this to occur are going to do any better job in the management of organizations in the private sector.

Still another sanction that exists and is frequently employed is that of public relations. Both the press and the better informed citizens the press produces are much more attuned to what is happening than ever before. An organization's violation can have repercussions of a very serious nature to its public image. Depending on the nature of the firm, this can have serious consequences. The severity will depend on the nature of the product and the market involved.

Most organizations have come to recognize the need for positive public relations if they are to continue. Large organizations have recognized this and have gone to the use of experts by setting up public relations departments. Unfortunately, many smaller ones have not invested in professionals in this field. The task usually falls to the senior executives and to the area assigned the responsibility for administering the program affected by a specific body of legislation.

In our case, this means that the responsibility will fall on the personnel department. Even in large organizations, personnel must coordinate with and assist the professionals in public relations to achieve an appropriate program. Again, we note an expansion of both the function and power of personnel.

LENGTH OF LEGAL IMPACT

Will these legal constraints continue to impact on personnel—meaning labor laws, affirmative action, ERISA, and OSHA? The answer to this frequently creates criticism from all sides. Many feel these laws will not go away, and, in the broadest sense, they are correct. The laws are with us and are not going to be repealed. However, the intensity of the problem, as with any problem, diminishes over time. When OSHA first came out, it was the major concern for those in personnel at the time. There was rumor, confusion, contradictions, varied interpretation, etc. This then gives way, after approximately seven years, to a period of understanding, which will last for an indefinite period of time. The final phase is the ultimate demise, replacement with another, expanded version, or inclusion in a broader sense. These phases are pictorially shown in Fig. 4-3. The problem is they will be replaced with new legislation.

Those who are in the position of having to take action in the very beginning pay the greatest price. They are the trailblazers, and the test targets for the regulatory agencies. Precedents have not been selected and benchmark decisions have not been made. This is the most difficult period to the organization caught in the middle.

An organization that can wait it out and is not forced into immediate action during these early turbulent years will have a much easier time implementing the program. They have the benefit of trading on the experience of others. Later on, outside help is available for pur-

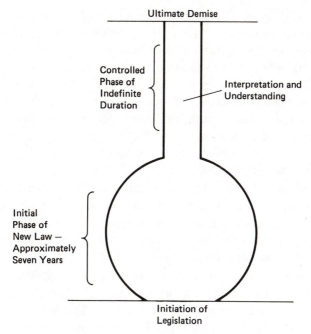

Ultimate Demise

Controlled
Phase of
Indefinite
Duration

Interpretation and
Understanding

Initial
Phase of
New Law —
Approximately
Seven Years

Initiation of
Legislation

Fig. 4-3. Legal impact.

chase (e.g., consultants, training programs, etc.). In fact, one way to tell the phase that an issue is in is by looking at the availability of training programs and consultants on the topic in the marketplace. These increase over time to the point that when an issue is in its final stages, experts are everywhere.

WHAT MUST A PERSONNEL SYSTEM PROVIDE?

Legal interpretations are frequently many years in coming. A system is designed based on present knowledge. Herein lies a real problem.

If we design today's system, it may soon become obsolete. In every system design, this has to be a basic concern. However, the changes mandated through legislation or a court decision are not going to be optional. In fact, the length of time they can be postponed is usually limited.

When initially putting together a system, everything that seems reasonably feasible should be included. Then, those items that weren't thought of or generally aren't of major significance have to wait for the next system revision. This can be months or years away, depending on the size and complexity of the system. Our options are not this flexible where a legal requirement is involved.

We may not be able to wait for the next scheduled or anticipated revision to make the change. A special system revision has to be made to meet a mandated completion date. To make matters worse, this change may not be the only one. Right after it is made, a new law or court decision may require another special revision. This can be both disruptive and very costly.

The one way to fight this is to recognize that it can, and will, happen. Regardless of the effort to identify the possible data elements and report requirements, it must be recognized that they will be changing. This change may not occur in reasonable time frames within the scope of our knowledge at a specific point in time.

The name of the game is to achieve a *flexible* system. In today's environment, this has to be a paramount goal. There are a number of steps that can be taken to help achieve this. The first step is to assure that we can add data elements. If all of a sudden we have to start reporting to the government on height, color of eyes, and number of unfilled teeth, this can't be done without the ability to add these fields.

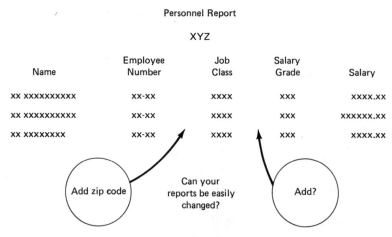

Fig. 4-4. Report flexibility is a must.

A system must be designed for significant and unexpected data elements that aren't even conceivable at the present. Some of the items that must be captured and reported today would have sounded ridiculous several years ago. Some say the best way to make this selection is to hold a brainstorming session and provide for the items that seem absolutely absurd.

The next area that must be provided for is that of reports developed from the data element base. Figure 4-4 shows the common problem that most reports run into—the need for flexibility. No report is everlasting, but many designers approach them as if they were. This is analogous to painting oneself into a corner.

Reports should be treated as if their format will be obsolete the day they are produced. Taking this approach is logical and is good insurance. The saddest thing is a report whose format can't be readily changed. It will soon be obsolete and supplemented with so many supporting reports that a bigger problem will result.

5
DEFINING THE DATA ELEMENTS

Earlier, it was noted that defining the data elements is an important first step. This is possibly an understatement, since the data elements are the "heart of the system." Not only defining them, but properly defining them, may be the single most important step in designing the personnel system. It is unfortunate, but this is one step that is often either overlooked or done in haste with little care.

WHY THE DATA ELEMENT DEFINITION IS FIRST

Reports will come and go, be modified and changed, etc. They are temporary and, as previously noted, probably obsolete before they come out. At most, they are a transient item in the personnel system. Too often, we find that these same reports are used by those designing the system as the basis for the structure of the new system. They erroneously use the old reports as the starting point.

Suppose a person was building a new house because the old one was deteriorating. They certainly wouldn't want to see the builder start by nailing new boards onto rotting timbers. In fact, they would want to start with a sound foundation. If some of the previous material was usable, they might want to include it. They would probably save some of the antiques and family heirlooms, if these fit in with the new decor. They would not use the rotting timbers or crumbling foundation as their starting point.

The same thing is true of our personnel system. There may be some things that we want to save, but if we are building a new system, a new foundation is a logical first step. The foundation of the personnel system is the data element structure. This will dictate what can or cannot be included on a future report.

The first phase of the process is to obtain a list of existing data elements. Remember that the existing reports are only one source. A second, and more difficult, part of the process will be to obtain a written definition. The data elements must be defined to the satisfaction of those who must see them.

What is the point of this written definition? Probably the most important thing is agreement—agreement by everyone involved as to what the data elements individually mean. This assures that none are overlooked and that people fully understand those that are included. Putting this down in writing allows them to be circulated and reviewed.

The review and agreement must come from all levels. A frequent error is to get the approval only at the upper echelons. We want to involve as great a number of people as is feasible. Those who are going to be working with the data elements on a daily basis are of particular importance. They have a vested interest in the way the system operates. It is from this source that the most attentive and detailed review is made.

After the existing data elements are identified, we want to expand and do the same thing with the new data elements we will be adding. Some feel that old and new data elements can be identified and defined at the same time.

It may be easier to keep them initially separate for a couple of reasons. First, there is a lot more effort needed in identifying and defining the existing data elements than one would assume. The actual amount of work in this step is not readily apparent until it is well under way. Secondly, the process of identifying new data elements is more creative in nature. We are asking people to think of the new or future system and to temporarily forget about the existing one. This brings into play a different set of skills and techniques. Trying to focus on old and new at the same time may stifle some of this creativity.

This leads to the question of how we get people to think about the new data elements. There are various approaches, from group brainstorming to individual interviews. The one thread in both cases is the need for an outside facilitator, someone to act as a catalyst to get the ball rolling and keep it rolling. This is one area in which a survey form does not work very well. A certain amount of individual contact is required.

One of the most effective means to get people to talk about what is needed in the new system is an individual one-on-one interview. The size of the organization may dictate that a team of interviewers be used to cover everyone involved. It is appropriate to develop a standard set of leading questions beforehand. Examples of these might be items such as: What information do you need that you aren't getting? What information will you need if we add product line *X, Y,* or *Z?* Questions of this type set the atmosphere and the mood for some creative thinking.

USE OF EXISTING REPORTS

It has been noted that existing reports are not the place to start in identifying the system requirements. These reports for our purposes are history. They are a source of knowledge of what has existed in the past, but not of what will exist in the future.

Reports make it too easy to lock in on a solution to a few present problems, but detract from the main objective. If everything is satisfactory with the existing system, both now and in the near future, we are not going to be modifying it or developing a new system. We are taking these actions for the very reason that something is not working.

This theme has been deliberately repeated several times (even pictorially, in Fig. 5-1), the reason being that it is one of the most common errors in designing a personnel system, and has tremendous impact on the effectiveness of what is developed. We too frequently design an improved historical (obsolete) system. What we want is to design a system that meets our present and future needs. Proper data element definition leads us down this path.

SOURCES OF DATA ELEMENTS

Those who are going to use the system are going to be a good source. If they are presently using an existing system, they can usually tell you what they like and don't like about it. They may have some strong feelings about what they want to see in a new system that doesn't exist.

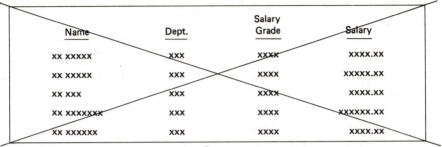

Report

Data Element List

1. Name
2. Initials
3. Department
4. Salary grade
5. Salary rate
6. Last increase amount
7. Payroll station
8. Work location
9. Shift, etc.

Fig. 5-1. Data element definition (not reports): The systems key.

These people are generally going to be parochial in that they see their own requirements and possibly only theirs. As you go higher in the organization, the scope broadens, but the ability to think in terms of specific data elements lessens. By the nature of the work, senior level managers deal in broad concepts rather than in specific technical points.

It takes a special talent to integrate the workers who have the technical needs and the managers who have the broad operating concepts. The systems analyst must be able to fill the gap and work in both worlds. The tendency, if not controlled, is to work in one area or another where a comfort level exists. Realistically, an effort must be made to avoid this and assure that all areas are adequately covered.

SELECTION OF THE SYSTEMS ANALYSTS

It is obvious that selecting people who have the talent and ability to be comfortable working with people at various levels is important. We can select one group that is comfortable with senior management and another that is comfortable with line employees. However, at some point, *someone* has to tie the package together.

Many people feel that analysts who can work in both areas to begin with are desirable. There is a need to integrate concepts and line activity on an ongoing basis. The whole is no better than the sum of its parts in this instance. This school of thought says that this on-going process is necessary to assure that proper system conceptualization, design, and development occurs.

Finding the systems analysts to do these tasks may be a problem. Most organizations immediately look to their internal staff and make a selection. Too frequently, these people do not possess either the technical or the practical experience to conduct such a project.

To begin with, the ideal analysts should have a dual background in personnel and in systems. If you look at the backgrounds of most internal teams, they bring in some people with backgrounds in personnel and others with a background in systems. Both then have to go through a long learning period to pick up the missing discipline.

An immediate problem exists in that there often isn't time for this learning experience! Then we may wind up with a team that can't work together in a cohesive fashion. Some will argue that a good systems analyst can acquire the skills/knowledge of personnel rather rapidly. The concept that this feeling exists may be indicative of the fact that the personnel function is viewed in its old light. That of being a simple recordkeeping function, rather than the present complex discipline that can't be learned overnight.

The next mistake that is frequently made is not to insist that at least part of the team has past experience. Just as in battle, green troops make more mistakes, have higher casualties, and lose more battles. The mistakes in a major system modification or design can be very costly—costly in dollars and in time spent "reinventing the wheel."

A person who has been through *not just one,* but several, similar system studies can be worth his/her weight in gold—both literally and figuratively. If the study team is large, including the experienced resources is not enough; they must be positioned so that the information they have to share can be heard and acted upon.

We too often take a valuable resource and then bury it in the organizational structure. Later, we wonder why nothing was done and why this person didn't contribute! Knowledge and talent do not necessarily carry the attributes of being aggressive. In fact, one may cancel out the other. It is a wise administrator who recognizes this and acts accordingly.

PURCHASING NECESSARY TALENT

What do you do when you don't have people with the skills mentioned? The wrong answer to this (and the one most frequently given) is to make substitutions with the hope that they will learn over time. This accounts for poor performance exhibited by hastily and ill equipped in-house teams. The blind end up leading the blind.

The option that is frequently overlooked is that of using outside consulting assistance. This can be for the entire team, or just for the areas of expertise not available in-house. This is one way of building depth into the study team that would not otherwise be available.

Too often, this is written off by the organization as being too costly. Granted, there is an immediate outflow of payments to a consultant. However, there is a comparable, yet less visible, outflow for the payroll of the internal staff.

An inexperienced internal staff can actually cost an organization significantly greater dollars. Mistakes can be very costly, and may result in additional unscheduled revisions. The time involved is another significant factor. The inexperienced take longer to do the project, thus increasing the number of payroll dollars involved. In some cases, this alone exceeds the cost of the consultant by multiples of five or ten.

Most systems are being modified or redesigned with little, if any, lead time. The problem is usually very real and urgent before the effort is approved and given the go-ahead. This means that the system *was needed yesterday*. The longer it takes to obtain the new system, the more the organization suffers.

There seems to be a long learning curve for inexperienced people working on personnel systems. It is not uncommon to see people working on a major system in excess of five years. No one envisioned this length of time to bring the system up, but it happens all too often.

This is very disheartening for everyone involved. Costs will be running five or ten times the original estimates, and an end product may not be in sight. It would have been much less costly to have gone to a consultant and have the job done by an expert in a timely fashion. They say experience is the best teacher, and most organizations have to experience a severe problem before they seek the necessary outside assistance.

DATA ELEMENTS EQUAL SUCCESS OR FAILURE

Figure 5-2 displays a personnel system continuum. If we think of the system in a historical sense, it is pictured as a series of reports. It is the sum total of what it produced. Like any historical event, we can see the beginning, middle, and end. Since it is in the past, we have a total overall perspective.

The current system operating now is viewed differently, since time is in a different framework. We know what the current reports are and even some of the history of their evolution. The new projects that are presently being developed are limited or constrained only by the data elements available. Consequently, those data elements that were defined and included previously in the system dictate what can be done with the system today.

If the system was originally designed to allow for expansion of the data element base, there is an added dimension. We have additional options and expansion capabilities in the present. The system can grow until this capacity is exhausted. When it is exhausted, the system is obsolete and must be modified or a new system developed.

The future system is based on the data elements and structure established at the time of development. This becomes the mold that sets the outer limits. The most difficult part of this process is to concentrate on the future needs. The tendency is to think about what

	Historical System	Today's System	Future System
Bases of the System	Reports	Current Reports and Data Elements	Data Elements

Fig. 5-2. Personnel system continuum.

was (history) and what is (the present). What also needs to be focused on is what is to come (the future).

We won't be working in the past or present with the new system, but in the future. The system must provide for these data elements. It must provide sufficient flexibility to add newly defined data elements. This assures a long life and avoidance of the common problem of the system's being obsolete before or right after being put into operation.

The success or failure of most personnel systems comes during the data element definition phase. A system designed to meet historical and present needs is doomed to rapid obsolescence and failure, for this is not the time period in which it will be employed. On the other hand, the system designed to meet future needs will be successful. It is in the future that we must live and work.

FUTURE DESIGN TECHNIQUES

Obviously, the design team must be future-oriented. This is not easy to achieve. Those who must work with the future system are probably working with the present system. Their knowledge of what the present system does not do is valuable. However, they also have a certain attachment to the present system.

Everyone resists change. All people seek pleasure and avoid pain. Systems usually change only when they become very painful. We change them very slowly, and hang onto those parts that give pleasure with a vengeance. There is a very strong tendency to be defensive and very protective regarding the parts of the old system that still function adequately.

This is hardly the setting one would hope for when trying to stimulate a creative environment. However, it is the setting that we are normally going to be confronted with. Therefore, it is the one we must learn to work with. One of the first steps may be to recognize that some of the team members, if not all, are going to have strong feelings about preserving certain aspects of the status quo. Recognizing that a problem exists is always one of the major steps in solving it.

The data element definition approach supports this premise. Data elements are neutral in eliciting emotional response when compared to, say, reports. Reports can be identified or benchmarked against the present or historical system. An attempt will be made to preserve those reports or parts of reports that are still found to be useful. This can be a block in designing the future, for we must mentally leave the historical and the present.

With data elements, we can incorporate and define those that will be needed today with little problem. The compromise is small; the future is not mortgaged. It is this freedom to be creative that makes the use of data element definition so valuable.

6
DEFINING THE REPORTS

The definition of reports has its place in the sequence of steps. In previous chapters, we have specified it as an important step, but not as the first step in developing a personnel system. The reports need as their base a fully developed and defined set of data elements. This assures that the system will meet current and future demands on it.

REPORT REQUIREMENTS

Reports are a picture or snapshot of an organization's information requirements at a single point in time. They are a fluid and an ever-changing item in the organization's communication chain, not a final step. Report design is not a place to create a lasting monument or establish some form of organizational immortality.

A report may meet today's needs and have to be completely re-formatted tomorrow. A report should not be designed as if it is a final solution. Then, when the organization needs it changed to meet the changing operating requirements, a problem develops.

The individual or group responsible for the report becomes defensive. A request for change can create hostility. It is taken as a personal affront to the designer's work. This occurs when all that has happened is that the organization's communication needs have varied according to a changing environment.

This problem must be confronted very early by those involved in designing or modifying a personnel system. Resistance to change is not going to go away, but it can be recognized and, in some cases, provisions made to ease the impact. When the report is first discussed with the user, the concern is usually with today's needs. A good analyst must be aware that these will certainly change over time. The process is ongoing and evolutionary, and this recognition is important, since it affects report design.

REPORT DESIGN

The reports must also be designed for the user and not for the analyst. At first glance, this would seem to be so obvious that it need not be mentioned. However, in actual practice, few reports ever meet the user's requirements.

If you would like to test this, take a recently designed report and distribute to users response questionnaires similar to the one in Fig. 6-1. The results will normally be shocking. Most users did not get what they wanted. They have compromised to get at least part of what they needed to do their job. Additional changes need to occur before their original requirements are met.

Why does this happen? There are several reasons. One of the most common is scheduling. Personnel systems seem to always be behind schedule in development. It must be remembered that the real push for development does not occur until the situation has become critical. Management generally procrastinates in approval until major problems are being experienced. Hence, when the system is approved, those involved are put under extreme pressure to get something done very rapidly. The need is at a critical state.

Another reason is the act of "taking a snapshot" of the system at some point. The user is dealing with information and knowledge of yesterday's problems and requirements. Changes and corrections to accommodate these are provided at the time these questions are asked. Then a lag lead time occurs until the new reports are prepared and out. This may range from a few months to several years. Herein lies a very real problem.

The organization has not stood still at this point. It has continued to evolve. The user gets what was discussed and previously approved. Unfortunately, the present and future states of activity dictate additional changes based on a different point in time.

If the system design is truly flexible, these report changes can be accommodated. This theme of flexibility in design of a personnel

Return to: (name and mail code)

User Report Survey

Control numbers:_____
Date sent:_____
Date returned:_____

Report name: _____
Report number: _____

1. Does this report meet your overall requirements?

     ☐ Yes   ☐ No

   If no, please indicate problem: _____

   _____

   _____

2. Would an added modification make this report more valuable?

     ☐ Yes   ☐ No

   If yes, please indicate modification: _____

   _____

   _____

3. Other comments you might have regarding this report: _____

   _____

   _____

   _____

   _____

   _____

Fig. 6-1. User report survey.

system is very important. It is the focal point for all aspects of the system. Nothing in the area of personnel systems is static. This creates a need and awareness of design flexibility. Without it, we have painted ourselves into a proverbial corner. With it, we have some-thing very exciting—a system that is not obsolete and one that meets the user's needs.

System design is not the same for different disciplines. There are many areas where, once a system is in place and defined, it can func-tion for a period of time without change. Personnel systems do not fit into this mold.

MANAGEMENT REPORT REQUIREMENTS

Management is involved in problem solving and day-to-day managerial activities. Managers know what they want on a report to solve an immediate existing problem. The nature of their work does not gen-erally make them good sources for what a specific working report should look like.

A manager must respond to a given problem. Also, a large portion of his or her time is spent receiving information from subordinates and passing it along to higher levels of managers or, vertically, to peers. This activity is depicted pictorially in Fig. 6-2.

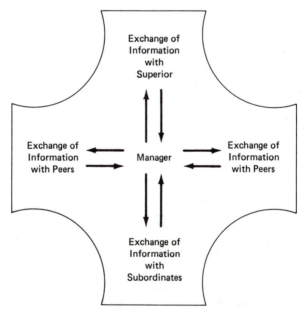

Fig. 6-2. Managerial communication funnel.

Managers deal with information and will be good at defining what is needed in reports—right? Wrong! As managers' needs for information to respond to a specific situation change, the formatting for a report to satisfy their needs changes. This can occur in a very short time—even in a few hours. Once again, the theme of flexibility comes through.

EMPLOYEE REPORT REQUIREMENTS

Employee or line report requirements are different to a certain degree. These are usually focused on the information required to perform a specific task or function. Usually, the information is static for a period of time. The information requirement does not usually vary, since an entire task or function would have to change in the process.

There is also a difference in scope. The employee who will use the report information in performing a line task does not have the broad perspective of management. In this case, the focus is usually on a part of the larger system. Significantly, for the analyst designing the report, the employee's focus is much more detailed and knowledgeable regarding the specific data elements involved.

Someone who has to use a report daily, weekly, monthly, etc., to perform a task soon knows it in detail. If he or she does not know the entire report, at least the portion used in detail is known. This can be valuable in report design, since the source generally has strong feelings about exactly what is needed. These usually cover what is needed right now and what would make the job easier, if additionally included or deleted from the report.

This information source can be valuable, if its limitations as well as its strengths are kept in mind. The employee is usually limited by not having the broad overview. This makes it difficult to tie the parts together or conceptualize the overall picture. On the other side of the coin, the employee has the detailed knowledge of the system. It is the analyst's job to bridge the gap (this is shown in Fig. 6-3).

OUTSIDE REPORT SOURCE INFORMATION

We should not be limited to the organization's managers and employees in defining our reports. Granted, they are excellent resources, but

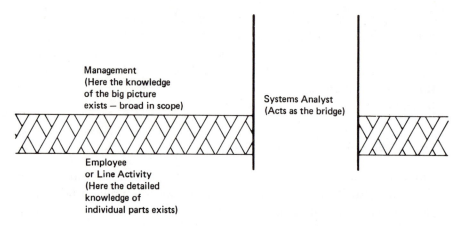

Fig. 6-3. The part of the analyst.

we too frequently stop with them. Defining reports should be a type of "shopping." People don't go to one store to do all of their shopping. Neither should they only look to their own organizations in establishing their reports. There are other resources that can provide valuable insights.

Stimulating creativity can be very important in report design and development. Most personnel departments deal with consultants and vendors for various services in employment, compensation, benefits, etc. If an outside consultant is not already employed in designing the personnel system, one might be considered, since a consultant can provide a wide range of information and experience that probably is not available internally.

Setting up a series of reports can be a trying experience. Those who have done this before know many alternatives, shortcuts, and enhancements. Their counsel and guidance will go a long way in helping an organization to avoid unnecessary repetitions of work that has already been done. Also, since they have previous experience, they can reduce the time involved in performing the task.

Whether using consultants or not, it is always wise to see what other related organizations have done. Personnel systems are normally not confidential items even between competitors. There is generally a willingness to share information, since people tend today to have more loyalty to the profession than to the particular organization. (This openness and sharing exists on information regarding systems, but not on specific information on individual employees or groups of employees.)

Most people do not effectively use this resource because they don't feel comfortable in asking others for systems information. There are several approaches to this. First, they may wish to use a consultant, as discussed earlier. A survey of related organizations may be one of the first assignments requested of the consultant. Another vehicle for learning what reports a related outside organization uses is the professional membership. One of the major objectives of membership in professional groups is information exchange. Belonging to a personnel professional club or society may be the avenue to find out what sister organizations are doing. They provide a contact point and an introduction. Some of the larger ones even provide research facilities and resources of their own.

THE IDEAL REPORT

Conflicts and differences result as to what information to include on each report. The analysts find that people will utilize the same report for multiple reasons. This means that they must investigate the various users to assure not only that the needs are met, but that the appropriate report is being used.

A report may meet the needs of the existing users. However, this is frequently short lived. Soon, changes and additions are required as business activities evolve. The greater the number of users, the sooner a single report is outdated and in need of change.

The local data processing group (if the system is automated) or business systems group, starts receiving numerous requests for changes. The more reports, the larger the organization, and the greater the number of users for a report, the faster this occurs. The entire system becomes overloaded. The organization becomes panicked and reacts.

The next step is to form the standard "priorities committee." This is usually composed of one or more people responsible for changing the system, and some senior members from the users side of the house. The purpose of this group is to sort through all the requests and determine which must be done first. There will be so many that a backlog will create a "log jam."

The real reason for the priorities committee is that the organization must be formally told that it can't have what it wants and needs. There is safety and a certain amount of authority in numbers. The priorities committee's basic function is to formally and officially say "no."

This is hardly the best solution, but it is one that is often employed. It does buy time, but only by stalling. If valid needs are not met, peoples' jobs become difficult. Pressure will finally be brought to revise or modify the system.

The system's modification will alleviate the immediate problem for a short time. Then it starts over again. As the new system ages, it may again no longer meet the user's needs. These start to pile up, and the priorities committee is reactivated.

Is there any way to stop this vicious circle? The answer is "maybe," and it lies in having a report system flexible enough to meet user needs. This flexibility in report design is of critical importance to any personnel system (this is shown in Fig. 6-4).

Problems occur when the user's report requirements can no longer

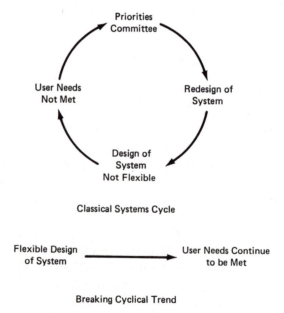

Classical Systems Cycle

Flexible Design of System ──────────▶ User Needs Continue to be Met

Breaking Cyclical Trend

Fig. 6-4. Breaking the systems cycle.

be met. These requirements change because personnel is not a static function but one that is growing and evolving. The reports must be able to parallel this change.

A viable report generator or report writer may be ideal for computer-based systems. It allows the creation of reports as they are needed. This is of particular significance if the people in personnel have control of the report generator (or writer). They can modify, change, add, or delete items to the reports as required. The more simplistic programming languages are allowing the user to have this capability. The user's ability to make changes as needed is the only answer to avoiding the normal report obsolescence problem.

The ultimate in user control will come with voice programming. Here, the requirements can be communicated without extensive computer language training. Only the users know what they need and their true priorities. Give them the ability to make their changes without relying on a third party, and many of the existing problems will disappear.

There are many names for putting the work back into the user's hands—decentralization, user control, distributed processing, etc. The meaning is the critical issue and not what label we hang onto it. This is to get the control into the hands of the person or group who have to use it on a daily basis.

WHAT ARE THE LIMITATIONS OF SUCH A SYSTEM?

A major concern is that the user has the necessary technical training to modify the reports as necessary. The user-controlled system without access is of little value. Hence, proper training and follow-up are essential.

All users in a specific group don't have to be able to individually access the system. However, sufficient numbers in the group who are considered part of the work team must have this capability. It is important that the group is in control of the system and related report changes. This control should be felt not only physically, but psychologically.

Another important limitation that was discussed previously is the data elements. Reports cannot be produced, modified, etc., if the appropriate data elements do not exist. They must be available, or the system must be designed so that they may be readily identified, captured, and added.

Data elements are the fuel that run the personnel system. This is why their importance has been emphasized. Ideally, we need to have not only those identified that will be required when the system is installed, but those that will be required in the years to come. It is here that obsolescence can be avoided.

All systems are technically capable of being decentralized. The trend is in this direction, and the technology is available to provide this capability. Internal politics can be more of a problem in this area. With user control, power switches from one area to another. Those whose power is negatively affected are justifiably concerned. Organizational politics is probably the single most important factor in slowing the movement to full user control. Data processing groups do not want to see personnel running their power bases. This is not a popular concept to put in writing—but it is highly realistic when viewed in the political environment that exists in every organization.

7
FORMS DESIGN

Forms are of importance to most administrative systems, and they are of critical importance to a personnel system. Some aspects of the forms in a personnel system are even controlled by law (e.g., questions on the employee application with affirmative action implications).

Forms serve as a device to capture and feed information into the system, and they may be the output from the system after processing has taken place. They are a major expense item when all aspects of their use are taken into account. Hence, they are significant from both an operational and a monetary point of view.

HOW MANY FORMS

What is the correct number of forms for a personnel system? Some operate with twelve or less, and others have two hundred. Obviously, there is a wide disparity in the use of forms.

Systems differ in size and complexity. Many people immediately assume that larger systems automatically need more forms to operate. This philosophy holds that forms are a function of size. However, if we look at various personnel systems, we will find that some of the larger ones are able to operate with fewer forms than those of lesser size. We do know that reducing the overall number of forms may reduce the operating costs of a system (see Fig. 7-1). Organizations frequently look only at the per unit cost of forms. Costs are examined on a reorder basis—$0.06, $0.35, $0.65, etc., each.

The cost per unit is really very small in comparison to the usage costs. A five-part form with carbons may cost a great deal more per

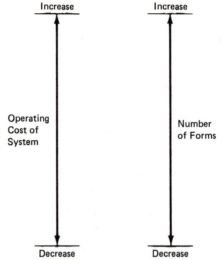

Increasing or decreasing the number of forms will affect
the overall operating costs of most personnel systems.

Fig. 7-1. Forms versus operating costs.

unit than a single-page form. However, the single-page form may
require so much handling within the system that these costs far out-
strip the per unit value.

Forms gather costs as they proceed through the system. Each form
must be initially filled out. Usually, there has to be a written procedure for doing this. Even if the completion of the form is not complex, there is a tendency to document its existence and use.

Elaborate files are soon set up to accommodate new forms. Those
who don't trust master files start setting up their own files. All of
these systems require additional time and cost. Add a new form and
these support systems will soon arise, thus compounding the costs
involved.

We all know people in our own organizations who maintain elaborate filing systems of every item that crosses their desks. Staff additions may be justified simply to maintain these systems, and these
additions become difficult to challenge since there is a visible volume
of work. In fact, they are hardly ever challenged, since a ready alternative may not be apparent.

BOOTLEG FORMS

One answer that is too readily jumped at is to cut the number of forms used in the personnel system. Forms cost money to order, fill out, handle, file, etc. Obviously, it is thought, if we reduce the number, we can achieve substantial savings in operating dollars. Unfortunately, this is only partially true.

Cutting the number of forms will only reduce costs if the information needs of the users are fully met in some other way. If the information is needed, eliminating the form will only reduce productivity. Only if the information is not needed will the elimination take place without causing operational problems.

A technique that is often used is to tightly control the addition of new forms. All forms are required to go through a central area for approval and formal acceptance. This works only as long as the system meets the organization's need for information. When it fails, unofficial (or bootleg) forms start to appear.

These bootleg forms are frequently rough drafts photocopied on in-house copying equipment, rather than coming through a supplier. They are not pretty or polished, but they are meeting a very real need that the formal system does not. They are also just as costly (frequently, more costly), for the printing is just a small portion of the cost of a form.

Bootleg forms leave the organization without standardization and general forms control, and, for several reasons, they are usually more costly than regular forms. There is apt to be duplication in development, design, storage, etc.; reordering any necessary supply can be difficult; and those who prepare the forms may do so in a confidential or semi-secret manner, since most organizations frown on bootleg forms, so if one of the "major suppliers" is absent, or leaves the organization, obtaining a new supply can be temporarily impossible.

How do you stop bootleg forms? The only way is to meet the needs of the organization with approved forms. Bootleg forms are symptomatic of a larger problem—the system itself. The major concern of an analyst is meeting the organization's needs. When this is accomplished, the problem will be self-correcting.

We don't want to *control* bootleg forms. Instead, we want to control the *reason* these forms are in existence: the demand for information that is not formally being met. When the demand is met, bootleg forms will disappear.

INPUT FORMS

Input forms are the ones that capture the data to go into the file. These are usually of two basic types. Those that provide initial data capture, and those that update or correct information already on file.

In personnel, one of the most basic input forms is usually the employment application. This is where the basic information package is started for an individual. The length of the application seems to be decreasing in the United States. Many personal questions regarding religion, race, family origin, and marital status can no longer be asked, since they may result in hiring discrimination.

Supplemental status change forms account for most of the increase in information captured. Though irrelevant information about people has been reduced, job-related data after the person has been hired is definitely on the increase. History files on job/salary progression, skills inventories, and performance ratings are but a few examples of the proliferation of information in this area. A large number of forms has been developed to support the data in this area.

The secret of good forms management is to balance keeping the number of these forms down with meeting the organization's needs. Good planning and frequent review in this area are essential. It is not uncommon to find an organization in which the personnel forms number into the hundreds. This should never have been allowed to occur.

OUTPUT FORMS

The area concerning output forms is just starting to get attention with the advent of the 1980's. Figure 7-2 depicts this change. In the past, we have focused the resources on developing systems for data capture, processing, and storage. We normally did little *creatively* regarding the output.

This has left a broad gap in both the use and the availability of information for managers. Time and money have been devoted heavily to the processing activity, possibly because the processing is fre-

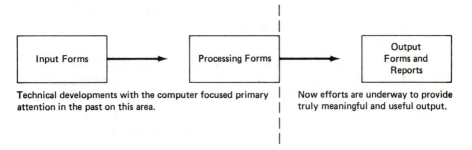

Fig. 7-2. New focus of attention for forms.

quently computer-based.   This area has been under heavy research and development.   The input portion has also received attention, since it fuels this activity.

Too few resources have been available to do justice to the output of the system. This portion has been designed not for the managers/users, but to satisfy the technicians designing the system. Forms and reports coming out of the system have not been meeting the requirements.

The secret for good output forms is, first, the form (or report) must provide the information the users need to perform their function, and, second, it must be in a format that is readable, functional, and pleasant to use.   Our output today more frequently meets the first requirement but has a long way to go in meeting the second.

Output media are varied, with a broad selection, though they are somewhat limited in manual systems.   The selection is becoming wider in the automated system.   A few examples of the options include preformatted form paper, standard computer paper, microfilm, video display, and the spoken word.

This wide variation has both pluses and minuses.   The analyst involved must study the needs of the various user groups.   A system must be tailored to meet not only group needs, but individual requirements that may be unique to a specific task or function. Once again, we see the ever-present theme of flexibility.

TURNAROUND DOCUMENT (FORM)

A very useful technique is to combine an input and output form, creating a "turnaround" document. This eliminates the need for having two separate forms. It also provides the person with space to make a change or a correction in the information regarding the present status of the information on which he or she is working. Figure 7-3 shows a sample turnaround document (form). The sample is in three parts. The first part shows the turnaround form with the preprinted information as it exists in the master personnel file. Then, when it is determined to make a change, the second part shows this change. The shaded area marked "correction or change" is where the data to be corrected or changed is indicated. This form becomes an active input form. It is sent into the system to activate the update process for the master personnel system. Finally, the output is a new form with the correction or change now indicated replacing the prior information. This output form is now ready to serve as the input form when another correction or change is necessary.

The user of this document can greatly reduce the need for researching and typing up information on an input document. This is partic-

1. Portion of original form

NAME	EMPLOYEE NUMBER	SHIFT	HOURS	PAY RATE
R.L. Smith	34531	2	8	$9.45
Correction/change data				

2. Change is made

NAME	EMPLOYEE NUMBER	SHIFT	HOURS	PAY RATE
R.L. Smith	34531	2	8	$9.45
Correction/change data				$11.00

3. New input/output form received, ready for future correction

NAME	EMPLOYEE NUMBER	SHIFT	HOURS	PAY RATE
R.L. Smith	34531	2	8	$11.00
Correction/change data				

Fig. 7-3. Turnaround document (report or form). The object in this sample is to change pay from $9.45 to $11.00.

ularly true if it is computer-produced, since all of the data is pre-stored and can be rapidly printed out much faster than a typist could.

Even in a manual system, there can be a time saving with a turn-around form. The information is put on the future input form at the time the change is fresh in the minds of those processing it. Since the processing of the correction or change normally takes place when updating the master records, salient information is readily available. Special research does not have to be conducted just to obtain such common items as name or employee number.

In the field, the user does not have to make great preparation for a change. The only areas that need to be filled in are those that are to be modified. There is not the standard petition of putting in the data for identification purposes that is going to stay the same. This is already on the form.

Security over the system of changes and corrections need not change. The same authorizations may be required and expected. The only time security and related signature authorizations need change is when a regular system study so indicates.

Special consideration has to be given to the storage and availability of the turnaround form. It is of little use if it can't be located when it's time to make a change. In a large organization, some forms are going to be lost or misplaced. This certainly has to be provided for if the system is going to work.

Either the central processing unit or the line has to be able to create a new document for replacement. The ideal way seems to be to have the line or using organization manually prepare missing documents. This tends to assure careful maintenance and storage of future turnaround forms received. However, this may not be possible if the line doesn't have access to the data necessary to recreate the document. This capability will vary from one organization to another.

CONTROL OF PROCESSING

If the personnel system is automated, there are generally problems in obtaining the forms processing desired. Usually, data processing controls the means of production, and personnel is but one of many clients or customers.

It also must be remembered that personnel is considered an overhead unit. Line or income producing units usually have priority.

This creates friction and there is always a priority battle underway, of one form or another.

One solution is to give the major data processing customers (including personnel) their own computer systems. With the advent of minicomputer systems that can be tied into a central or main computer unit, this has become feasible. Rather, it is feasible *technically*, but there may be political problems. Control and power shift under this situation, and this almost always causes problems.

Regardless of the political problems and obstacles, the trend is to place control of input, processing, and output back into the user's hands. This may occur at several levels, as shown in Fig. 7-4. As the control switches, so does the option to use various types of forms.

Each level has to exert control for daily operation. Forms are designed to allow for approval as they pass through each area, as well as to provide local processing instructions, control numbers, etc. Pass a form through enough areas and levels of control and it will either be illegible due to various added markings, or unwieldy in length and width. However, as control is returned to the user, the levels are re-

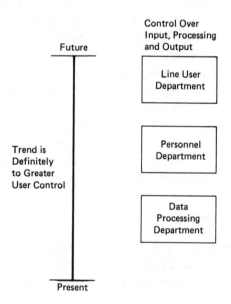

Fig. 7-4. Trends in automated user control.

duced. With this, comes a reduction in signature and other control markings.

USER PRINTERS AND INPUT DEVICES

One of the first steps in obtaining some semblance of user control is being able to print output in the user's area. Even without having a minicomputer physically within the area, a dedicated printer starts to show what autonomy can offer. The users begin to feel that they truly are part of the activity.

If, in addition, the user is given an input device—which can take the form of a card reader, a terminal, etc.—even more autonomy is felt. Of what value is this? If the user is directly involved and has some control, a new level of responsibility and involvement is achieved. The computer is no longer the only villain when something goes wrong.

Proximity and speed of delivery are also major concerns. Large computer centers have been developed that have centralized main data processing resources. Getting the input, and, even more frequently, the output, from or to a personnel site can be a problem.

Reports and printed forms can be "time dated" for use. There is often a great deal of work to be done on them, decisions to be made, signatures to be obtained, etc. A good example might be salary review documents that have to go through a long cycle of consideration, review, and approval before being input into the system. Getting preprinted salary review forms out and to those involved can be critical in returning them to meet payroll period cutoff dates.

Many organizations are decentralized, with operations over wide areas. Some operate internationally, with sites across borders and around the world. It is not always feasible to have printers located with the user. However, where it *is* feasible, this can greatly speed up form processing and turnaround.

In certain instances, user-operated input devices can be an advantage, though those controlled by the user are frequently slower and handle less volume than those at a central service center. The trade-offs in both areas should be weighed.

Some people feel this type of user-operated input/output for report and form processing is limited only to large organizations. Vendors and service bureaus that handle smaller organizations can provide on-site input/output services. These can currently be obtained for reasonable rental or lease fees. Operating need and not size should be the only concern.

IMPACT OF PERSONNEL HAVING ITS OWN COMPUTER

A consideration made possible by advanced technology is the concept of distributed data processing. Personnel departments can now consider having their own computer systems.

In large organizations with many decentralized locations, these computers can be tied in with the central computer. At night or during slack periods, the computers in the field can send back transactions that have occurred during the day or during any specified time period. This allows those in the field to operate their own computer—input, processing, and output. At the same time, a central (or corporate) data file is maintained. This allows production of any and all corporate and consolidated reports.

Outside of the politics of "who controls what and where," the next critical point in this type of operation is the skills to operate it. If personnel is to have its own computer capability, it must be able to technically support it. The skills to do this are not the ones normally associated with "personnel types."

There seem to be two ways we can approach and solve this problem. One is to hire or transfer people with the desired technical background into personnel. The other is to take selected people presently in personnel who show an interest and provide them with the necessary training. In practice, some of both is usually done, and this actually provides a better mix. Having people from within personnel, as well as new people with proper technical skills, seems to work out well. It gives the group a depth of knowledge in both areas.

Security of the data is frequently raised as an issue in allowing areas to have their own computer access. Regardless of safeguards, increasing the number of units increases the possibility that something can go wrong. The problem may be one of magnitude.

Personnel data is sensitive. Classified salary information (just one example) in the wrong hands can bring on all kinds of problems. Everything from employee unrest to lawsuits are potential hazards in the mishandling of personnel information.

We sometimes view the computer as making crime or unauthorized release of information easier. Of course, as information is computerized better, more accurate data handling occurs. But whether unauthorized access is easier might be a questionable point.

It takes a certain additional skill level to operate most computer equipment, and not everyone has it. Also, special internal audit controls and access codes usually protect most confidential files. It takes special skills and training to penetrate a computer system.

We may have a heightened level of fear because we are dealing with something new. Look at any personnel system that is not automated, and also at the reports and forms produced from an automated system. How are they filed and stored? What is the security on the desk drawers and file cabinets in which they are kept? Better yet, what about the tables, desktops, and file cabinet tops they usually are scattered on?

The point being made is that most forms and reports in personnel really have little or no security. It takes little skill or training to jimmy open a desk drawer or a file cabinet. You normally don't have to go to these lengths, anyway. The keys, assuming the drawers are actually locked, are normally "hidden" in a convenient place. A master set is usually in the possession of several people anyway— in case someone gets sick.

Computer security is important for personnel information. We shouldn't blow it out of proportion, though, to the safeguards taken in non-computer systems, or when the information is no longer in the computer. With this perspective, more rational decision-making can occur.

WHO IS THE USER?

We have talked about the "user," "personnel systems," "the line," etc. But *who* should have a computer system? Who are the people who should have their forms and reports printed out right in their own area?

Those of us who are in personnel usually consider ourselves the "user." However, by its very nature, personnel has traditionally been a staff group providing service to others. We generally handle large numbers of input/output forms and reports.

If the truth be known, these other groups would probably like direct access to their own personnel information. Their justification for having such access is no different than personnel's. This must not only be acknowledged, but should be considered as a viable future alternative. If personnel does not put people directly in the field to service what the line needs, then we need to anticipate the line requiring its own support.

PAPERLESS FORMS

The use of the cathode ray tube (CRT) or video screen has brought about a new dimension in forms. The CRT has a typewriter keyboard and a television-type display unit. This system has become quite popular for use within personnel units.

There may be times when you want to view information (or even make changes to data) and a piece of paper is not necessary. A good example might be viewing someone's start date to verify employment for a telephone inquiry. There is no need to have a hard copy form or report with this information on it, if you can view it on a television screen.

The CRT is ideal for displaying a form directly on the screen and then proceeding to fill in the necessary information. The typewriter terminal allows the information to be typed directly onto the form on the screen. This is almost identical to typing a form on a typewriter. In fact, with a CRT, you can have certain advantages over a typewriter, such as a wider view of the form and easier erasure.

The CRT has other advantages, such as pre-edits. Information that is not appropriate can be screened out as the operator tries to enter it. This allows the operator to take corrective action immediately, rather than (as with a standard paper form) having it sent back for correction days or weeks later.

For example, assume a terminal operator attempts to input the department number of an employee as 619. This can be checked by the system against the allowable table file for department numbers. Assume that department 619 is not allowable for several possible reasons—e.g., there is no such number, or it is not an appropriate number for certain job classifications. The number is not accepted, and the terminal operator is notified via a message on the screen.

This pre-editing has in itself a number of advantages. The time in catching and correcting an error is significantly reduced. If a paper form has been processed through the system, it might take days or weeks to catch the error, notify the necessary people, and take the proper action. Even more important, erroneous information is simply kept out of the system. Instant feedback has alerted those at (or closer to) the source of the possible future problems.

This proximity to origin gives another incentive to the use of CRT systems. Why forward a paper form past the input point? In a strictly paper system, forms flow past or through large numbers of people and usually come to rest in a file. With a CRT, a paper form may be used by the operator to originally transcribe the information, but then it can be filed. It stops at the input point and does not have to go through a massive handling process. Figure 7-5 shows this reduced flow.

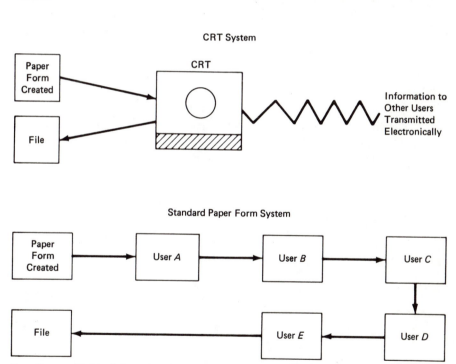

Fig. 7-5. Reducing form handling via CRT.

Not only is the paper flow reduced, but the information can be programmed to flow to other users much more rapidly. There is also less chance that the original document will be lost or misplaced: a significant savings from multiple points of view.

8
MAKE OR BUY DECISIONS

The question of whether to make your own personnel system or to buy one was touched on earlier. Why dwell on this topic? The reason is that, in today's marketplace, it is possibly the single most important decision in establishing or maintaining a personnel system.

Very few people realize the broad range of options open to us in the market to purchase a complete personnel system or portions of one, or just to consult aid to think through various portions of related problems. Most organizations have preconceived ideas about a very limited range of choices.

Too many organizations have fixed ideas and believe they can only go in one direction. Some feel their only option is internal creation of the system. If someone suggests buying a system or part of a system they just scoff. They are certain the costs would be too high. Then they proceed from scratch, and overrun their budgets by many multiples.

The horror stories on developing or modifying a personnel system are legend. Standard approaches to business decision-making seem to be ignored. Very often, business logic and the related body of knowledge seem to be replaced by preconceived ideas and strong emotions.

ALTERNATIVES IN PERSONNEL SYSTEMS

The first question that always arises is: "Are there alternatives?" You may also hear a surprised question: "There *are* alternatives?" In designing a personnel system, there are indeed many alternatives available to every organization. A few will be so applicable to a single organization that it will normally require some applied business research to select the most advantageous one.

There are always at least three choices available in this decision-making process. First, we can decide to "do nothing" about a new or modified personnel system. (Taking no action is an action in itself.) As pointed out before, we can always buy a system or make one. However, this is just the beginning of the alternatives open to us.

Figure 8-1 shows a few of the possible steps we might take. We start with a "do nothing" option and proceed in the example through a few of the make or buy combinations. This chart is certainly not exhaustive. In fact, it is only the beginning of a whole range of choices.

For example, the figure does not even begin to touch on the use of a third party expert—a consultant. We very well might want some outside assistance to evaluate the "buy decisions," the "make deci-

	Alternatives	Cost ($)	Consequences
1	Do nothing		
2	Make		
3	Buy		
4	Make 20% Buy 80%		
5	Make 80% Buy 20%		
6	Make 50% Buy 50%		
7	Etc.		

Fig. 8-1. Alternative selection chart.

sions," or combinations. Also, we might want more than one expert's opinion at various stages. As can be seen, the combinations and permutations are almost *in*exhaustible.

Each organization should establish a series of alternatives applicable to its situation. One way to do this is through a brain-storming session with a group of key managers. The best way to do this is to bring the group together for, say, an hour, when they won't be interrupted. Tell the group that no alternatives will be considered "stupid" or "ridiculous." In fact, the wilder the idea, the better. No one is to do anything but submit ideas. There are to be no evaluation comments regarding any ideas submitted.

At the session, all ideas should be recorded for future reference. No names of who made which suggestions should be noted, since to do so discourages input and may bring politics into play regarding future selection of possible alternatives. The result (or output) of this session should belong to the group and not to a single individual.

In another session, at a different date, the group may wish to go over the alternatives suggested in the brainstorming session. Some of the ideas that sounded wild may actually be practical. In this session, evaluation is acceptable, since the aim is to reduce the list to a practical number. Normally, the group will be able to do this quite well in this second session. The emotion is reduced and separated from the original idea-generating session.

Once an acceptable list of alternatives is established and agreed to by those involved, the next steps can be taken. One of the first will be to identify the costs of each. These can be rough at this stage. Where the "buy" consideration or the use of an outside consultant is contemplated, we may want to contact a few of these suppliers or consultants to get rough estimates. It is wise not to rely on our own judgment or on someone from inside our organization for this estimate. As noted before, many organizations automatically assume astronomical charges from outside sources. This, more often than not, is not the case.

We also want to identify the consequences of various alternatives. For example, if we use internal resources to develop the personnel system, these may not be available for another project. Not doing the other project may have substantial repercussions.

Both costs and consequences must be taken into consideration when evaluating an alternative (see Fig. 8-2). The least-cost item is

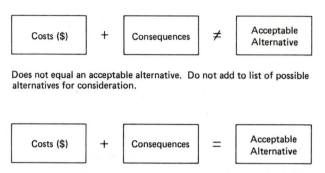

Does not equal an acceptable alternative. Do not add to list of possible alternatives for consideration.

Does equal an acceptable alternative. Add to list of possible alternatives.

Fig. 8-2. Acceptable alternatives.

not always the one selected. It must be least-cost *and* have the most acceptable set of consequences.

COST FACTORS INVOLVED

Often, a buy consideration is looked at in dollars and cents differently than a make consideration. Many organizations feel they aren't spending money if they make something internally. Those holding this philosophy may only be defending themselves in actual practice.

Internal resources should be assigned their true value. There are very real costs associated with using internal resources. First, if the resources are people, there are salaries involved. Then there is the hidden payroll dollar or fringe benefit involved. In the United States, this can equate to 20% or more of the payroll dollar. Examples of 40%, 50%, 60%, or more are not uncommon for some organizations. This can quickly add up.

Salary plus fringe benefits is not the whole story. Each individual tends to generate other operating expenses—travel, supplies, telephone, etc. Depending on the type of organization and work involved, this can easily exceed 50%.

Putting all the factors together (Fig. 8-3), we can see that an individual can cost more than the payroll dollar—sometimes even more than double the payroll dollar. Numbers such as these can have a sobering effect on the way we look at internal resources. We always have alternative projects they can be used on, or we can reduce staff. Hence, internal resources are not a "free ride."

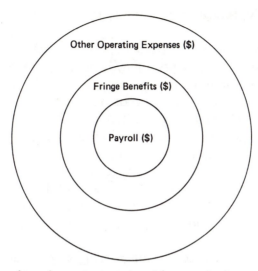

An employee generates more costs/expenses than just
the dollars we pay him/her.

Fig. 8-3. Employee costs.

Internal and external (make or buy) systems must be compared
based on the actual costs involved.   Availability is a relative item.
Cost must be accurately measured and comparisons made to determine the appropriate direction.

MANAGEMENT SUPPORT

Does management have preconceived ideas about external resources?
Can these be changed or modified? If the answer to the first question
is yes, then the answer to the second question is yes as well.

Unfortunately, the very nature of organizational structure does
not foster an open exchange of ideas and information. People spend
large portions of their time trying to second-guess what management
wants, and to have it ready when asked for it. If displeasure was ex-
pressed about a given idea or concept, it is avoided by the "troops."
These are, without question, survival techniques.

In reality, this behavior benefits neither the organization nor its
management. Ideas and creativity are stifled in this type of an environment. Options and alternatives become almost nonexistent. All

too frequently, though, this is the type of environment people must function in.

How do we present the external option to a management that may not be supportive? The answer may lie in using the factors that management focuses on to let the concept sell itself. What are these?

They can vary from organization to organization, but most frequently they will come down to dollars—either dollars that increase income, or dollars that reduce expenses; ultimately, dollars that have an impact on the operation of the organization.

If we look back as to why management did not want to consider an external source, it was probably because of dollars. It was felt that the external (or a buy) decision would, by its nature, be "too expensive." Obviously, as long as this idea continues to hold, nothing is going to change.

Management is swayed by dollar changes. An idea or concept can be held only as long as it is considered financially sound. If the external decision meets this criterion, it should be presented in dollar terms. It will be found that management at all levels is a great deal more flexible than was originally assumed.

INTERNAL DESIGN

In previous pages, the external (or buy) decision was focused on. The primary reason is that it is so frequently overlooked, ignored, or not considered. This focus has almost been to the exclusion of the internal (or make) alternative.

There are some very real plus considerations with an internally designed or made system. These may come out as part of the alternative analysis looking at the tradeoffs between make and buy. Suppose that, for a given organization, the research indicates that the organization's requirements for a specific system or modification can't be met externally. Nothing meeting the specified criteria exists.

Assuming the criteria both realistic and feasible, others may have need of the same system or modification. This means that, if there are a substantial number of other people with the same needs, a market has been identified. Depending on the success of the design development, we may want to consider the future of selling what has been put together.

This concept has certain built-in appeal to management in other organizations. If this has been developed by a group in a related or sister organization, they feel more confident about it working well for them. Someone else has pilot-tested and worked out most of the major problems. The potential for it not succeeding has been greatly reduced.

Rather than developing a system that is an expense item, you might put together a system that is marketable and produces income. Of course, if it is designed internally, the resources must be available both to design/develop and to market the product. However, in putting together any new system, it is always wise to see if others might be interested if such a system is available. If you need it, chances are good that so will someone else—and, if so, they may be willing to pay for it. This can be an offset to the cost incurred.

Even if you decide to purchase outside assistance, you might want to retain certain marketing rights if it is determined that the system has outside value. Contracts for outside assistance in designing or developing a system should be written to protect your interest and contribution. Generally, if the system has value to you, it will have value to others.

People agonize over developing a system and go through a lot of work ironing the bugs out. Then, because they didn't protect their interest, someone else picks up either the entire system, or unique portions that have been developed. These are then sold to others at a substantial profit, none of which is returned to the original developing firm.

There may be no way to formally patent your system. However, you can have written agreements with those outside your organization who work with you. Also, and possibly more significantly, you can be first to the market with your package. Most systems that are appropriated and sold by others occur after a period of time has elapsed since development. Usually, after the system (or systems') has achieved success and a certain amount of notoriety.

The time to lay the groundwork for marketing your development is early, before its benefits are widely known. This early lead will frequently discourage those who might want to copy and sell what you have developed. Additionally, those who purchase the product would prefer to have the original, which you possess, rather than a copy, the reason being that the original has proven itself.

SECURITY AS A MAKE ISSUE

Organizations that are heavily security-oriented, either because of trade secrets or for governmental reasons, tend to develop their own systems. A highly secret environment is conducive to this type of behavior. Exchange of information is usually a two-way street. Thus, those in a more secret environment don't ask for fear of being asked for something in return.

Personnel systems developed in such an environment tend to spend large amounts of time on problems others have already solved. Without a substantial line of communication with others, this is going to be inevitable. How can this be overcome?

First, we want to be assured that the security environment is necessary in the area of personnel systems. People who work closely with security may automatically assume that it applies to all areas. It may be that it is applicable only to a selected engineering or laboratory area, and the secrecy value has permeated the remainder of the organization. If it is not mandatory, then we are free to contact and use various outside information resources without being concerned.

Let's assume that security *is* a concern, and that we aren't free to openly deal with outside firms, vendors, etc. Are there any options? Yes, possibly several. Most organizations' security groups have lists of approved outside resources who have been granted clearance. Also, there are procedures available to gain approval for new resources.

The point is that, even where security is a concern, we can still avail ourselves of the latest innovations. Understanding this is vital in avoiding needless repetition. No single organization contains sufficient internal resources. Outside contact and study in one form or another are very important in obtaining a personnel system that will meet an organization's needs.

9
EMPLOYMENT SYSTEMS

The employment functions and who performs them will vary by the size and philosophy of an organization. In a small, single proprietorship, only one individual may be involved, while in a large organization, such as government, hundreds or thousands may be involved.

In its broadest sense, the task of employment is to fill vacancies. This can mean internal placement as well as hiring from the outside. The objective is to match people with the proper job or position.

PARTS OF AN EMPLOYMENT FUNCTION

The functions that can be assigned to employment are varied. A sample list is shown in Fig. 9-1. The list, of course, is not all-inclusive,

Employment Administration
Salary or Professional Recruiting
Hourly or Clerical Recruiting
High School/College Recruiting
Transfers
Job Posting
Skills Inventory
Replacement Pool (Temporary)
Employment Records
Applicant Testing

Fig. 9-1. Employment functions.

but it provides a guide to the major areas to be considered. The larger the organization that is serviced, the more definitively the functions will be broken out.

In the example just cited, a large organization would probably have the functions listed spelled out as separate entities. An administration section would be available to coordinate and manage the various functions.

Recruiting would very probably be specialized, as noted in the example. Separate recruiters would handle the salary or professional hiring, and another group would handle the hourly or clerical level activities. School recruiting (high school and college) is given special attention because there is frequently heavy competition for these resources.

In a large organization, transfers take on very special significance. They are a valuable internal resource that does not require the training and orientation an outside hire would. The larger the organization, the more imperative that this aspect of placement become formalized. As an organization grows, this resource automatically increases in size.

Closely related to, and frequently a source of internal applicants, is job posting. Here, open positions are posted on bulletin boards, or made known through other means, for employees to bid on. This gives the employee interested in a new position the option to review open jobs before going to other sources or to the outside.

Visibility within large organizations is a must both for management and employees. Skills inventories, either manual or machine run, aid in matching employees with positions. They are systems that aid in matching employees' experience, education, and preference with specific requirements to perform a given activity or function. Also, they are a useful tool in providing a list of potential candidates for a position.

Organizations with standardized jobs frequently form a temporary placement pool. These are people who possess the needed skills who act as "floaters" and fill in for those absent or on vacation. This precludes downtime, since the individual taking over the job temporarily is familiar with the task and the organization's policies. It avoids the learning curve of an outside resource. Examples of temporary pools might include secretaries, tellers in banks, and draftsmen in engineering firms.

Employment records often are not given sufficient billing as a separate entity. Because of the volume of applicants for a single position, the recordkeeping function can be substantial in even a small organization. Affirmative action programs require identification and detailed recordkeeping to assure that applicants aren't discriminated against. In addition, active resume files need to be maintained, response letters to applicants filed, etc.

Applicant testing is a function that has had its ups and downs. Affirmative action has dictated that tests must be psychologically validated to assure that they are not biased against or in favor of certain classes or groups of people. Some organizations abandoned testing altogether to avoid possible problems. Now, many tests that have been validated for screening applicants are available, and a number of organizations are returning to the screening device, so this function is again increasing in importance.

EMPLOYMENT NEGLECT

Employment is often completely neglected from a personnel systems' point of view. Why is this? It may be that few people view it as a structured function. Another possibility is that it is so complex that many systems analysts find it easier to ignore it.

In another chapter, compensation systems are discussed. This is probably the other side of the coin, since compensation systems are much in use in personnel systems. It may be that the more structured or quantifiable nature of this function has led systems analysts to develop this area.

Employment is a function most people feel automatically qualified to handle. This is erroneous, since the activity is more complex than its name connotes. It takes an experienced professional to perform the function properly and in a timely fashion.

Many employment functions do not operate properly. Recruiters are overloaded, applicant files are misplaced, applicants aren't properly screened, and response time is slow. This is indicative of a very serious problem. Too often, it is just accepted as a standard part of doing business—but it is not and shouldn't be accepted as such.

What is wrong? What ingredient is missing? The answer is rather obvious—a personnel system for employment. If one were properly positioned, workload would be properly allocated, applicant files would be readily located, proper screening would occur, and adequate response time would be established. When an adequate system is in place, many of the overwhelming problems tend to disappear.

AN ADMINISTRATIVE UNIT

The function of employment is more than just hiring people— a lot more. It is the purpose of employment administration to integrate a series of activities. There must be a focus of control. The larger the organization, the more visible this need becomes.

A central unit must be responsible for the activities and the way they interrelate. When this is not present, the chaos results that so often depicts an employment function. Figure 9-2 shows administration acting as the central unit, coordinating the various functions. This assures that the proper ones are being performed, that there is no overlap or duplication, that items are not overlooked, etc.

A Central Location or Area Must Integrate the Activities

Fig. 9-2. Employment administration.

In an operation of any size, this activity should consist of more than just a manager and a secretary. It should possess one or more people with a systems background—preferably, a business systems background, people with the analytical training to measure the work, identify the work flow, and analyze and design the proper forms.

Traditionalists are shocked by this suggestion. Most employment functions are composed of people with skills in such areas as recruiting, interviewing, and selection techniques. Skills in the business systems area tend to be alien in such an environment. The question is: Should they be?

The answer may lie in the results desired. If we want a smooth-running operation and an end to the confusion, we may wish to look at this possibility. A new set of skills has to be achieved to solve the inherent problems, problems that are the direct result of not having the required skills to deal with the ever-increasing complexity in the employment area.

There are, of course, options on how this skill level can be achieved. One is to bring in someone from the outside, and the other is to train the existing staff. There are problems and benefits associated with doing either. The best way seems to be doing a bit of each, with an expert from outside used to train and work with the existing staff. This assures that the depth of knowledge regarding employment exists, while providing selected training in business systems.

RECRUITING SYSTEMS

As mentioned earlier, one of the problems in looking at employment is that we are not used to looking at it procedurally or in a systems vein. However, if something is done properly, there are certain steps taken to achieve this. Should these steps be repeated, logically, similar results should be achieved.

Each organization has its own set of steps for recruiting. These steps probably vary for different categories of positions. For example, there is probably one set of steps for clerical recruiting and another set for professional recruiting. Examples are shown in Fig. 9-3 (hypothetical clerical recruiting steps) and Fig. 9-4 (hypothetical professional recruiting steps). Larger organizations that have a substantial senior management structure will also have a third set of steps (Figure 9-5—hypothetical executive recruiting steps).

These steps will vary from one organization to another. Also, they may vary from one segment of an organization (e.g., plant, division, etc.) to another. The important factor is that they are identified and agreed upon as the procedures for a specific segment. Assuming that the group agrees to the most logical and efficient set of steps, the recruiting function is operating optimally.

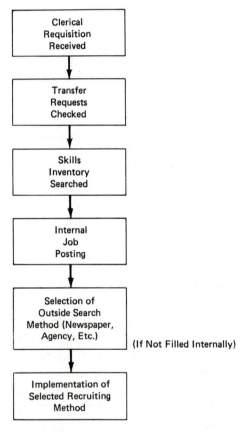

Fig. 9-3. Hypothetical clerical recruiting steps.

SELECTION SYSTEM

Ideally, recruiting does not produce a single candidate, but a group or list of candidates. If the recruiting system produces a single candidate, then it is not providing us a sufficient choice. It is operating as both a recruiting and a selection system. It is in the selection system where the list of candidates is reviewed and the single most qualified is actually selected.

If the recruiting system has done its job, a large volume of candidates have been attracted. The number of candidates we want will vary by a number of factors, such as the number of openings and the

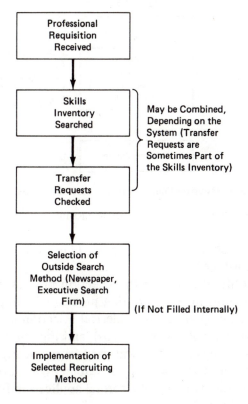

Fig. 9-4. Hypothetical professional recruiting steps.

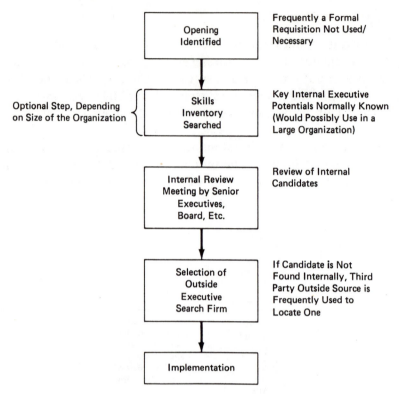

Fig. 9-5. Hypothetical executive recruiting steps.

type of openings (e.g., clerical or professional). We may want to review ten candidates for a clerical typing position, but only three for an engineering stress analysts's spot. (This will vary from one organization to another.)

There are identifiable steps in the selection process, just as there were identifiable steps in the recruiting process. Examples of these are shown in Fig. 9-6 (hypothetical clerical selection steps), Fig. 9-7 (hypothetical professional selection steps), and Fig. 9-8 (hypothetical executive selection steps). These will vary from one organization to another. They can also vary within units of an organization. A good example of this is the handling of a formal application form. A sample is provided in Fig. 9-9.

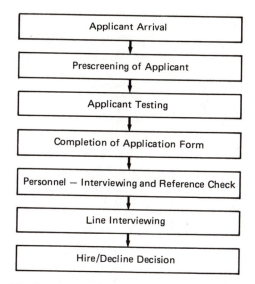

Fig. 9-6. Hypothetical clerical selection steps.

Some organizations don't even talk to an applicant until the form is filled out. Others don't give it to someone unless a decision to hire has been made. In the case of executives, it may never be completed. Executives are frequently exempted from completing application forms, or, if an executive is hired and asked to complete a formal application, the application is one of the last steps. Generally, a background investigation has been conducted and all the information on an application (and then some) is known. The application, if used at all, is purely a formality rather than an information-gathering tool.

A clerical application may be shorter than a professional application. We are not as concerned with formal education, past projects, or programs that the individual has worked on. Past knowledge and experience is not as important as present speed and skill.

As with the recruiting system, the important factor is recognizing that a selection system does exist. One should be designed to sequentially meet an organization's needs. The steps should be logical and in tune with both policies and objectives.

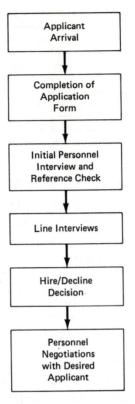

Fig. 9-7. Hypothetical professional selection steps.

SUPPORT SYSTEMS

A myriad of support systems must exist for the employment function to operate. These will also vary by organization. One that is common to most recruiting systems is the advertising support system. Another, also related to recruitment, is the search firm support system. These have been singled out here for further review because they both contribute high dollar expenditures (they are shown in Fig. 9-10).

The key questions in identifying whether such a system exists are: "When are they used?" and "Is there a logical set of circumstances

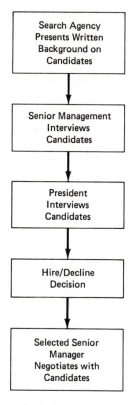

Fig. 9-8. Hypothetical executive selection steps.

that triggers the use of a search firm or a newspaper ad?" If either of these occur on a whim or an arbitrary decision by a recruiter, it may require a second look. This is indicative of a system not existing. If this is the case, money may be needlessly expended.

Not only is the expenditure of money involved, but the wrong recruiting source may be used at an inappropriate time. This can result in not producing the proper number and quality of candidates desired. This is another test for employers to see if the recruiting support systems are properly in place. Are there sufficient candidates to choose from for an opening? Is the quality (e.g., experience, education) of applicants at the level desired? A "no" answer could be indicative of a market condition *or* of an improper support system.

			Date		
			Month	Day	Year
Last Name	First Name	Middle Initial	Social Security Number		
Home Address (Number, Street, City, and Zip)					
Indicate any other names under which you have worked or obtained education					

	Name of School or College	Location (Number, Street, City, and Zip)	From Month Year	To Month Year	Diplomas, Degrees
High School					
College					
College					
Graduate Work					

List Additional Skills or Training

For Clerical Applicants	Types of Office Machines You Operate
Do You Type? Do You Take Shorthand?	1. _____
Yes ☐ No ☐ Yes ☐ No ☐	2. _____

Fig. 9-9. Sample application.

Employment for Last Five Years, Starting with Most Recent					
From Month Year	To Month Year	Employer's Name, Address	Phone (Area Code)	Your Position/Title	Reason for Leaving
			( )		
			( )		
			( )		
			( )		
			( )		

Have You Ever Been Convicted of a Felony? Yes ☐ No ☐	If Yes, Please Explain:
Have You Ever Had a Bond Canceled or Refused? Yes ☐ No ☐	If Yes, Please Explain:

I Understand Any Misstatements May Result in Dismissal.

_____
Applicants Signature

_____
Employment Interviewer

_____
Date

Fig. 9-9. Sample application (continued).

The internal placement system, which is frequently maintained in the employment area, is another crucial support system. It is important for a number of reasons, not the least of which is morale.

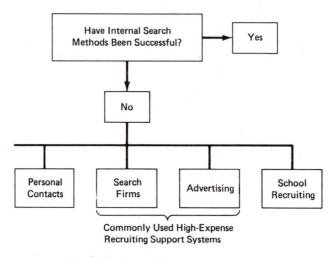

Fig. 9-10. Recruiting support systems.

Everyone wants to believe he/she is not lost or overlooked by the organization. Having an internal placement or transfer system can be an aid in this area. Ideally, through job posting and skills inventory support systems, all openings will be reviewed against internal possibilities before going outside.

Additionally, internal placement systems provide candidates who already know the organization. There is not the added training and orientation that is necessary to bring outside hires up to speed. Internal placements speed up the ability to accomplish specific tasks.

There are many more support systems within employment, as with any major area in personnel. Support systems can grow and evolve into major systems themselves. Also, what may be a support system in one organization may be a major system in another.

LEGALLY REQUIRED SYSTEMS

Outside forces have probably done more to bring personnel into a logical systems mode than anything else. Left to its own devices, personnel seems to be content to muddle along in a haphazard, unstructured environment. It is unfortunate that it sometimes takes legislative action to bring about an ordered and logical approach. In the long run, we pay for the loss of control and managerial prerogative that accompany government intervention.

Employment has its share of systems (or support systems) that are the result of, or are in response to, legislative action. The single largest impact on personnel in the United States has probably resulted from the necessity to respond to affirmative action requirements.

There are several areas in which this has had an impact. One is in the tracking of applicants. Many organizations keep detailed records of those people who have applied for a job, whether or not they actually were hired.

These records contain such information as sex, minority code, estimated age, whether the applicant handicapped or not, etc. The reason for this information is to meet, and defend against, charges of discrimination in hiring, or to be prepared should a compliance officer ask about hiring practices in a routine investigation. Collecting and storing this information on each applicant (not just hires, but those who only apply) is expensive and time-consuming.

Though the costs are high, this is the only way to adequately show that hiring practices are not discriminatory. The burden of proof is on the employer, who must show that he/she is not discriminating. The only way to do this is to capture the data elements that are necessary to prove that hiring is impartial.

Another employment area that can come under third-party scrutiny is testing. Using tests as a screening device is perfectly acceptable as long as they are valid. They must not be discriminatory and they have to be job-related.

When affirmative action first started challenging testing procedures, many firms stopped testing completely as part of the selection process. For a period of time, only certain tests (such as typing) were all that remained. The trend seems to have reversed itself as testing experts have "validated" tests and made them available in the marketplace.

Those concerned about the legality of the tests they are using have several options. They can go out and purchase tests that have been validated, or they can purchase the services of a testing expert to validate existing tests. They may use such an expert to develop new ones that are approved. With the options available, tests are now, once again, becoming an acceptable part of the selection process.

PROPER SELECTION — A RETURN ON INVESTMENT

There are definite costs involved in bringing people into an organization. There are the immediately obvious costs that have been discussed in this chapter—primarily, recruiting and selecting. In fact, if we didn't have to replace people, the cost of the entire employment area could be saved. This would be a substantial saving for most organizations.

Later we shall talk about training and development costs. These costs are significant for anyone brought in from the outside. Not only is there a learning period and the unproductive time of the new person, but there is also the unproductive time of the managers, and of peers who must give of their time and energy to do the instructing and answer questions.

We too readily take these training and development costs as part of doing business. They are, in fact, variable costs that are controllable. Since they can be large for a given organization, any reduction can account for substantial dollar savings.

There is a very real expense incurred in turnover of staff if we have to replace departing employees. If the firm is managing down in staff, and does not replace people who leave, there is no problem. However, if a new requisition is sent to employment as soon as someone gives notice, there may well be a problem.

There are many reasons for turnover, and one that employment people should be aware of deals with selection. Have the right people been matched with the proper jobs? Are people leaving soon after hire because the job didn't meet their expectations? Were they promised something that did not come to pass?

We could go on with a list of questions such as this for pages. The significant point, from employment's point of view, is turnover of recent hires. This can be a few weeks or a few months for hourly or clerical employees. Professional and managerial employees may last longer—a year or two. In both cases, early turnover may be indicative of mismatching. It certainly should be explored.

EMPLOYMENT DATA ELEMENTS

The importance of data elements was stated earlier. One of the first steps in setting up a system or a series of systems for employment is identifying these. One way to do this is by functional groupings.

Earlier in this chapter, we identified some basic employment functions—e.g., employment administration, salary or professional recruiting, hourly or clerical recruiting, high school and college recruiting, and transfers. These are not "set in concrete," but will vary from one employment operation to another. They can, however, be identified within each organization.

Every employment area has its unique group of functions that have been assigned to it. These provide a target area from which the analyst can obtain the data elements. These areas will definitely have duplicate data elements, but they will also have some unique ones specific to that function.

10
TRAINING AND DEVELOPMENT SYSTEMS

Most personnel departments have the responsibility for training and development to some degree. There are organizations in which this activity is separated from personnel and operates under a separate administration. However, the "classical organization" chart will show this function under personnel.

In actual practice, it is difficult to assign the activity specifically to anyone because it is so broad in scope. Every good manager must be constantly involved in training and development. (This is depicted in Fig. 10-1.) Whether the line organizations show it on their formal organization chart makes no difference. They still must provide for it if they are to be effective.

Thus, it is almost impossible for personnel to have all the training and development activity reporting to them. In a large organization, the best that can be hoped for is to be identified as the "centerpost" or area for administrative control. The range and scope has to be broad to meet the organizational needs. Having personnel as the centerpost can avoid duplication of existing instructional activities, facilities, and materials. It gives the organization a central area or group whose responsibility it is to know what is going on and where it is occurring.

WHAT IS TRAINING AND DEVELOPMENT?

Just getting your arms around the definition is difficult. There are a myriad of reasons for this, one being a disagreement even by professionals involved as to both definition and demarcation as to when these activities begin or end.

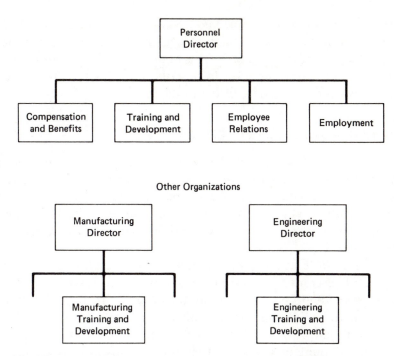

Fig. 10-1. Training and development in classical personnel unit.

The definition of training and development is a much-argued point. Training is often viewed as consisting of the specific skills that can be imparted to people. The term is often associated with blue collar or hourly paid clerical employees. Development is often interpreted as the method of acquiring knowledge over time. It is often applied to the professional or managerial ranks.

These definitions seem to be always open to challenge and disagreement. The primary reason may be because of the implied status involved. Dealing with "managers" or "professionals" carries more weight than "blue collar," "hourly" (etc.) workers. Couple this with people's ego needs, and a definition problem exists.

This is readily identified by the fact that different organizations call it by different names (employee development, staff development, etc.). Those reading this can probably come up with eight or nine examples of their own.

This "creative naming" probably satisfies some egos, but it creates a communication mess. When you say you are referring to compensation or employment, people know what you are talking about. The name identifies the basic function performed. People will usually ask, "Do you mean training?" It is hoped that, at some future date, we will all agree on one term to describe the activity. In the meantime, it is good to be aware of the problem.

TRAINING AND DEVELOPMENT FUNCTIONS

Regardless of what we call the activity, the functions involved are important to any organization. A possible function list is shown in Fig. 10-2. Of course, this list can, and will, vary from one organization to another, and even within different areas of the same organization. Functions will be added and deleted as the working area's needs dictate.

The list starts out showing a training and development administration. This control function is always prevalent, though not always specifically identified. Even in an operation consisting of only one function, there are still the administrative chores to be completed. Those who have worked in the instructional area can readily identify with the amount of work and time involved in this very significant activity.

Technical training is shown as a separate functional entity. What is actually performed under this title will vary widely from one organization to another. In a manufacturing/engineering area, this usually will consist of training for the shop personnel (e.g., welding, lathe

Training and Development Administration
Technical Training
Management Development
Executive Development
Career Development
New Employee Orientation
Outside Education
Educational Resources
Instructional Audit

Fig. 10-2. Training and development functions.

operation), while in the area of service industries, this may deal with the growing need for clerical skills (e.g., word processing operating, bank teller jobs).

Management development covers a very wide range of possible interpretations, too. These can range from basic supervisory classes to complicated interpersonal skills. Some define management development as instructional efforts aimed at any individual group who supervise or manage others.

Executive development is also open to various definitions. This category usually is reserved for the more senior level managers in an organization. The term "executive" is often abused and misused, as are all titles signifying status. Organizations often use titles in lieu of compensation to reward people, or to impress clients or customers. The true "executives" almost have to be separately identified on an organization-by-organization basis.

Career development is a function we are hearing more about these days. More and more organizations are providing the tools to assist employees in identifying where they want to go and how to get there. Achievement in one area may require sacrifices in another. The first step in any growth process is to identify the goal, and then to review the needed steps from the present position. Many organizations are recognizing that such a program benefits both the employees and themselves.

Another function we are seeing more of, which is often attached to training and development areas, is new employee orientation. Organizations recognize that all employees go through an "orientation process." If such a process is not offered formally, then it is done informally by the new employee's co-workers (peers). Since this is the critical "first impression" received by the employee, most organizations are opting to structure and control this educational experience.

Figure 10-3 depicts some of the steps that can take place in the orientation process. Co-workers (peers) always influence an employee's perception of the organization. In the absence of formal organizational orientation, it is the only influence. Many organizations want the opportunity to present their position, since the co-workers may not always present the consistent picture desired.

Outside education can be an important item depending on both availability and dollars being expended on it. Due to improved com-

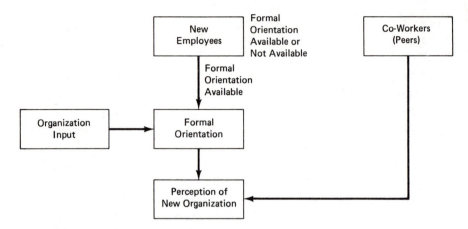

Fig. 10-3. Orientation alternatives. (Co-workers (or peers) always influence an employee's perception of the organization. In the absense of formal organization orientation, it is the only influence.)

munication and the increase in on-site programs, availability is not the problem it once was. However, cost is always a very real concern, and outside educational programs can be expensive.

Most organizations sponsor outside educational programs, and reimburse employees at least partially if not in total. These outside programs often are a major resource for both management and executive development. They also can provide courses and information that is more current and broader based than the internal organization is geared to provide.

A frequent function often found in training and development is the area that deals with educational resources. This area can provide access to audiovisual equipment, film library, material library, etc. It sometimes coordinates with the use of an outside consultant, which is a growing instructional resource. Courses and studies that aren't available through internal sources can often be purchased through a consultant or vendor in the outside market.

The wide range of choices and options in the area gives rise to the last function shown in the list. Instructional audits are becoming more important as the complexities grow. Here we find out whether an instructional program has delivered what was desired. This allows proper direction of resources into appropriate areas.

TRAINING SYSTEMS

Training is accomplished by the use of internal resources, external resources, or a combination of both. At any point in time, we generally have a fairly good idea of the capability of our internal resources—or do we? This is an oft-heard statement that contradicts itself.

Those resources presently involved in the training function are usually identified and accounted for. Most organizations have substantial resources within their ranks that aren't recognized. This is one area where a skills inventory frequently pays off handsomely. It can be the tool to aid in identifying a pool of people with the required skills and interests to perform various types of training.

The alternative to using inside resources is to go to an outside firm or individual. This may be particularly applicable for instruction in a new technology or one that is not presently used within that organization. Often, the knowledge would not be available in-house. The options here are to go outside, to hire a new instructor who possesses this background, or to send existing instructors for special training.

Most organizations tend to go for a combination of these, and rightly so. There can be many steps in a training system, as shown in Fig. 10-4. As with any example, it is not completely representative. However, the important point is the emphasis it makes on *resources.*

Too often, those in training (this can be broadened to include development) have had extensive classroom experience and immediately focus on the instructional portion of the system. This is a natural impulse, but it is costly. It is important to step back, away from the details, and take a look at the "big picture."

Part of the "big picture" comes into play early in resources. This is important because we limit ourselves if the complex options are not fully considered. For example, we may decide to have the need analysis done externally, part of the design done internally and part externally, the materials prepared internally, and the instruction provided by an outside firm.

DEVELOPMENT SYSTEMS

The same choices exist for the development systems. They can be provided internally, externally, or some combination of both. There

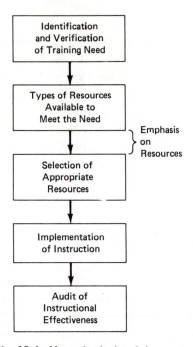

Fig. 10-4. Hypothetical training system.

is more dimension and a broader scope in the options open than are sometimes covered. We should not go for a quick solution without exploring alternatives.

For example, outside education seems to play a much larger role in development than in training. The time horizons of development are often viewed as being much longer or ongoing. There is no single class or course of instruction that imparts the knowledge a manager or executive needs to perform all of his/her functions.

To take this a step farther, there is even disagreement on the exact body of knowledge that would be useful. Even if there was some semblance of agreement on curriculum, it would have to be flexible and easily modified due to the rapid changes being experienced in every discipline including management.

These reasons have made many colleges and universities centers of management and executive training. The extremely large market for development has changed the traditional way many of these institutions operate. Time frames have been modified on several fronts to meet this need.

The traditional degree programs extend over many years and require periods of time on the campus. This time was normally in the eight to five mode. Immediately, a conflict resulted, since this is a prime time mode for managers to be at their work area.

In recent years, this has been changed to accommodate the broad need and market that was found to exist. Courses were arranged so that they were made available evenings and weekends by most major colleges and universities. Where these have been slow in coming in larger state universities, small private colleges have sprung up to meet the needs.

Newer modes of instruction have been (and are being) tested with some success. An example would be the use of broadcast and/or television cassette tapes filmed on campus and brought into the organization. This may better accommodate the time desires of both management and the colleges and universities involved.

Changes have occurred in the longer time horizons of degree granting—again, right or wrong, to meet a very real and lucrative marketing need. Those in academia often don't like to discuss this, since it smarts of the compromise of principles and scholarly excellence for monetary rewards. However, it is occurring and doesn't seem in the process of disappearing in the near future.

It manifests itself in several ways. One is the granting of educational degrees based on "life experience." In this case, work experience and related activity is counted in lieu of more formal classroom study. Another area is that of awarding of certificates. Students are provided with formal-looking pieces of paper with the completion of only a portion of the activity required for the award of a related degree.

Part of the development process may be formal recognition of one's efforts. Society and its values have changed, and people have little patience for an extended waiting period or apprenticeship. As the world moves faster, certain phases of development, including formal symbols such as degrees, have changed as well to meet the pace.

To be successful, a development system has to meet a broad range of needs. These include the individual's, organizations, and societies.

They are interrelated, and one is frequently dependent upon what happens to another.

DEMAND FOR TRAINING AND DEVELOPMENT SYSTEMS

Management is constantly requesting new and revised programs for their employees and themselves. To those trying to meet these needs, the task seems never-ending and the goal elusive. In reality, this is probably an accurate description of how management sees training and development.

Those seeking closure or completion rarely have their needs met. Unless the world stands still, training and development needs will continue to expand and evolve. Changes in world economy, technology, environment (etc.) constantly change the ground rules, as well as the tools with which organizations must work. These changes initiate the requirements for both different information and skills to perform in a changed arena.

The constant change and need for new and revised training and development programs sends out mixed messages. Frequently management, both inside and outside of training and development, justifiably becomes concerned about the effectiveness of the programs. Is the change indicative of not doing the job right the first time? How can we wrap up the program once and for all? Are we spending money and not receiving full value—or any value?

Each training or development system is unique, designed to fill a specific need or set of needs. These needs are constantly changing. Thus, it is very difficult to make a single study of effectiveness, as with many personnel systems. The target is moving, and must move to remain current.

INSTRUCTIONAL AUDIT

Many of the questions that arise with any training and development system are depicted in Fig. 10-5. The instructional audit is shown as a focal point, which is as it should be. In organizations where one does not exist, these questions are batted around constantly, or are studied one at a time.

Does the System Meet Employees' Needs?

Does the System Meet Requirements?

Is the System Responsive?

Instructional Audit

Are the Latest Technological Changes Covered?

Is the System Up to Date?

Is the System Returning Fair Value?

Are Revisions Timely?

Fig. 10-5. Answers provided by instructional audit.

An instructional audit system that is in place and fully operational will go far to resolve these. It will aid in answering questions for each training and development system. This is a preventive step that stops problems in the early stages, rather than allowing them to get out of hand.

A good audit system contains some basic components. First, records must be captured on who attended what course, when, and for what length of time. Any measurement of skills, learning progress, knowledge, etc., both before and after attending is of value. Keeping in mind that the ultimate objective is to rate the overall effectiveness of the training or development activity.

Details on establishing measures cannot be covered here, since each system is unique. Even a general review of measurement techniques could easily go into volumes. In designing an instructional audit system, the measurement area is one where a technical consultant could be extremely valuable.

Many systems stop with just identifying information and measurement criteria of the students and participants. It should be noted that we may want to include superiors, subordinates, and peers of those involved. Their observations may be of even greater value, since they come from a different perspective.

RESPONSIBILITY FOR THE DESIGN OF TRAINING AND DEVELOPMENT SYSTEM

This is a controversial issue, to say the least. It becomes more so as the organization grows in size. When it is small, people frequently understand the various functions and activities being performed, not only in their own area, but in the areas of their co-workers. With size, this, of course, is lost.

In a large organization, areas become highly specialized. Pockets of specialization obviously create a unique body of knowledge. When this body of knowledge needs to be expanded or passes along to others, training and/or development are involved.

One of the major problems that often arises is that of who is responsible for a training and development system. If the line people feel they are, and training and development people feel they are, there is trouble. The same thing happens if the opposite occurs and neither sees a responsibility.

In reality, both the line (or operating unit) and training and development people have vital input. Figure 10-6 shows the relationship pictorially. Both areas have parts that need to be put together to accomplish the objective. Bridging the gap is often not a small problem.

In the case cited, nothing will be accomplished in bringing a viable system up without mutual cooperation. The training and development department staff specialists bring the instructional expertise, the contact with outside resources, instructional support materials and equipment, etc. On the other side of the equation, the line or operating department brings operating experience, technical knowledge, access to technical support materials and equipment, etc. A marriage of these resources is necessary to bring a system into being.

How do we do this? There presently isn't an all-encompassing solution. There are, however, some possible approaches. One of the first steps is to recognize that the gap, break, division, etc.—whatever name you wish to give to it—exists. Line and staff functions have traditionally gotten along like oil and water. It may be better to confront this issue head-on, since denying it exists just seems to compound the problem.

In some cases, the head of the training and development activity has the personality to overcome this line resistance. In other cases, com-

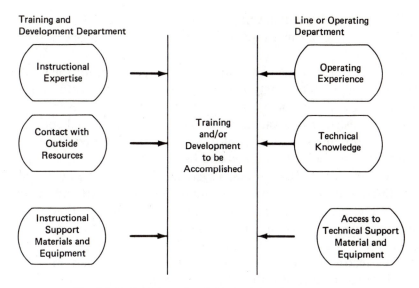

Fig. 10-6. Bridging of training and development gap.

mittees are formed to assure not only the proper allocation of resources, but to assure, too, that they work together in a compatible
manner. Frequently, a third party consultant, either internal or external to the organization, can be a tremendous aid in overcoming
the resistance and problems involved in getting the system up.

A third party is viewed as not having any axe to grind. They are
not viewed as part of the political intrigue that plagues all organizations. Double and triple meanings are not read into their statements
and advice. They are viewed as being there to help and bring appropriate parts together to get the system "off the dime." This can be
vital to avoiding or removing the stagnation and lack of communication that is often present. Third party intervention is not a panacea,
but it can provide the needed catalyst.

WHY TRAINING AND DEVELOPMENT SYSTEMS MAY BE ABANDONED

Often, we see a great deal of work by line, staff, and possibly third
parties to develop a system. Then it is used a few times, or not at all.
It may stay on the books for a period of time as an active available
system, but for all intents and purposes it has been abandoned. This
can be both demoralizing and costly.

Why are training and development systems sometimes abandoned? Obviously, there are many reasons (one very common one is shown in Fig. 10-7).

It is easy to get carried away and design any system for the sake of satisfying the systems analyst or designer. This is too often true in the training and development area. This occurs almost every time a system is designed in a vacuum without close contact and coordination with the line or operational user. They must be constantly on board if the system is to succeed and be fully utilized.

However, as Fig. 10-8 shows, a system can fall flat even with close coordination between the training and development staff and the line users. The information has to be current and timely. Frequently, there is a long lag lead time in the identification of a training system requirement and its actually being brought into operation.

Some instructional systems are time-dated. After a certain period, they become historical rather than having any current use. Others, particularly those not in a technically changing environment, are not affected by time. This relationship is shown in Fig. 10-9. They are just as valid and useful in implementation now as in several years hence. The only value that is lost is in the skills of those who didn't receive the instruction.

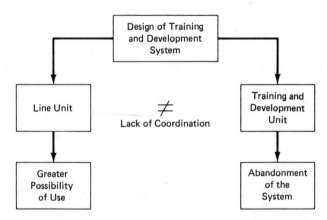

Fig. 10-7. System is not designed for the line unit. (Systems not designed for the line or operating unit are more apt to fail. Training and development units have to guard against design that is neither coordinated nor tailored for the user.)

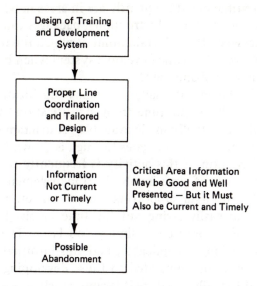

Fig. 10-8. System designed too late to be current and timely.

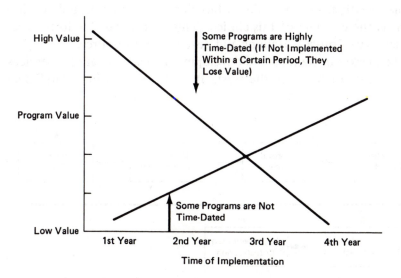

Fig. 10-9. Value curve in implementation of programs.

Those that are time-dated frequently are in areas in which technology is changing and evolving. Instructional packages can become obsolete or unnecessary after a certain point at which the technology is moved on. Why would anyone develop a system when it is no longer needed, just to have it abandoned?

They don't do this intentionally. In many organizations, there is "pipeline time." This is the time from identification of a need for instruction until it is actually made available. A diagram showing the possible steps or phases a project goes through is shown in Fig. 10-10.

The approval portion of this activity is frequently responsible for extending the amount of time involved. If management is uncertain or asks for follow-up data supporting a go ahead (etc.), the project approval phase can easily string out the time involved. In certain cases, the decision to proceed is simply too late. The training or development is no longer applicable, and this information is either not available or not communicated to those developing the system. It is programmed for failure before it is completed.

ALTERNATE TRAINING RESOURCES

Earlier we discussed the make or buy decision. Training and development is the epitome of this choice. This is probably due to the wide availability of outside training and development resources.

The market in training and development packages, tailored services, etc. is substantial to say the least. It is so large that in a "buy" decision one can be overwhelmed by the multiple options. Most training

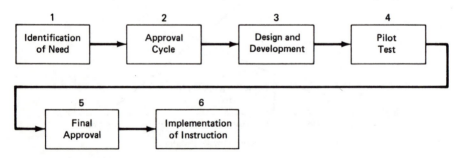

Fig. 10-10. Pipeline line in the instructional cycle. (Time is variable by project. It may be a matter of weeks or may extend to several years.)

and development directors and managers are literally inundated with letters and phone calls regarding such services.

This means that a very large training and development activity can be operated with little or no staff if an organization so desires. The outside services are here to meet any effort. The choice is up to the management involved. As stated in the chapter covering make or buy, the decision should be based on the logical business decision making steps. The important point being that in this area of personnel there is not scarcity of options.

11
COMPENSATION SYSTEMS

Compensation systems are considered by many to be the center of the personnel activity, with other systems being secondary. It may be that this argument is based on the fact that compensation systems frequently entail the largest dollar impact of any of the systems in personnel. Consequently, they rate highest in importance.

This, of course, varies by organization. The compensation activity is more significant in a labor-intensive activity than in a capital-intensive one. (This is shown in Fig. 11-1.) The reason is purely economics.

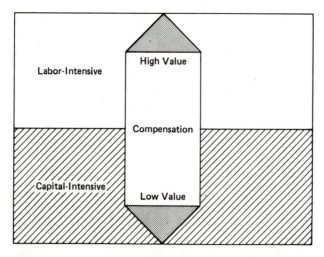

Fig. 11-1. Importance of compensation. (The importance of compensation increases in a labor-intensive organization and decreases in a capital-intensive organization.)

In a labor-intensive activity, a larger portion of the resources go out as compensation dollars to the employees.

Most organizations focus attention on where large dollars are spent or on where savings can be achieved. If the payroll is a large portion of the expenditures, compensation systems become of great importance, whereas in a capital-intensive activity, the emphasis may be on machinery, mineral leases, land holdings, etc., for this is where the large dollars exist.

FUNCTIONS OF A COMPENSATION SYSTEM

Figure 11-2 shows some of the more common functions of a compensation system. Administration is shown as the initial item on the list. Here is where policies and procedures are disseminated. This system acts as the central control to assure that the others are properly staffed and executed.

A system is needed to ensure compliance with state and federal wage and hour laws. These cover such areas as hours worked, minimum wages, and overtime. A system must be established, not only to track the data involved, but to adequately keep records. If a challenge is received — say, as to proper payment of overtime — the organization records must be adequate or they will be found in violation. The burden of proof rests with the organization rather than with the challenger.

Compensation Administration
Regulations Regarding Wages and Hours
Executive Salary Actions
Salary/Professional Salary Actions
Hourly Salary Actions
Policy Exceptions
Incentive Compensation
Salary Surveys
Job Descriptions
Job Coding

Fig. 11-2. Compensation functions.

Executive salary actions frequently are separated from other activity for a variety of reasons. One is usually the added security of
confidentiality extend to their treatment. Additionally, executives
may receive a varied compensation package that differs from the
others. This requires separate administration.

Salary/professional actions are usually administered differently
from executive and hourly employees. The differences may run the
gamut from treatment of overtime to pay scheduling (e.g., weekly,
every two weeks). Usually, the pay in this area is for doing a specific
type of work rather than for specific hours worked.

Hourly salary actions are frequently impacted by numerous forces.
These are often specified not only internally, but by government regulations, union contract, etc. Because of the various rules, agreements,
timing, etc., that may be involved, these may present one of the most
difficult systems to design and monitor.

Policy exceptions were noted as one of the systems to be included.
No compensation activity can adhere to policy and procedure in every
instance. Inflexible systems are, by design, doomed to failure. There
are going to be exceptions or variances and a system must be designed
to handle them.

Incentive compensation is a growing area for most organizations.
Previously, it was limited to sales personnel, or to areas such as the
garment industry for which piecework would be paid. Incentive systems are becoming increasingly popular, since they help in reversing
the decreasing productivity trend.

Salary surveys, though shown farther down the list, certainly are
not low in importance. In fact, they may be one of the most important systems or sets of systems in the compensation area. It is through
these that an organization determines its competitive position regarding compensation. These provide the basis to determine whether the
existing policies are adequate to meet the goals and objectives.

Job descriptions are a separate type of systems. Depending on how
they are prepared, they can give both a narrative and a quantitative
flavor to outlining what is being performed. The description can be
important in determining the worth of the position in comparison to
others.

Job codes have a varied connotation. Here it is defined as a system
to both more easily identify the position, as well as to describe the

value of the job in relation to others. This dual use greatly enhances its worth.

SURVEY SYSTEMS

One of the functions noted that needs a definite system to support it is that of wage and salary surveys. If not formally done by compensation at multiple levels, there will be constant challenges. It must be remembered that line supervisors and employees are constantly doing their own surveys.

Compensation not only buys material things, but is a measure of status. If people don't talk about it themselves, then their spouses, children, or friends will. When concrete data is not available to the various sources, it will be made up or estimated by those who want to discuss it.

When someone quits for another job, one of the first questions asked by those involved is where the individual is going. This is followed by subtle and/or direct probes as to the new pay rate. People who change jobs for less than a specific acceptable percentage, which varies with industry and inflation, are considered to have lost. Those exceeding this rate are considered winners.

An individual's social and professional standing can be tied up in his/her present compensation rate. If the employee changes jobs, this same measure applies. The worth of an individual, right or wrong, is intertwined in this number. It is society's measure of the persons contribution. One reason for this may be that it is one of the few quantifiable measures available to us in society.

If these sources aren't sufficient, there are a myriad of others. For example, labor settlements are frequently published in newspapers, classified ads may show dollars, and search agencies may inform employees of dollar possibilities. Thus, organizations that aren't aware of the current market are in a difficult position because their employees are constantly getting market input.

Those organizations that fall very far behind the market are in trouble. Since, even at parity with the market, there will be selected people who receive above average offers. It won't take long for this to reach the informal communication channels, and for people to start looking. If only a few exceptions exist, the exodus will be small.

However, if the organization is truly substantially below the market, a large exodus can occur quite rapidly.

One of the first decisions concerns what the market is. Figure 11-3 shows a sample of market considerations. Even though many are shown, the example is far from being all-encompassing. There are many possible markets.

Before a survey system can be set up, the organization must decide which market or markets it intends to compete in for its labor supply. These should be periodically reviewed, because all markets change and evolve.

If jobs are fairly specialized and related to a certain type of organization, it may be decided only to compete within that market. For example, a cosmetic firm may decide to compete with the rates of pay established by other cosmetic firms. Should aerospace pay higher rates for a similar job, the cosmetic firm would not try to match it. However, the decision of the cosmetic firm just to compete with other cosmetic firms has not totally limited its survey area. Geographical considerations for surveying come into play. Is it competing for talent locally, within the state, nationally, internationally? These factors might change the type and nature of the area to be surveyed.

What about jobs that aren't generic to a given industry? Many specialized organizations have data processing functions. Almost all

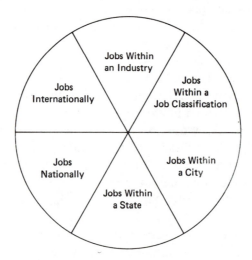

Fig. 11-3. Multiple markets for jobs.

the jobs in this area are used by other organizations in almost every field imaginable. Another example might be secretaries, which are used by every organization.

There may be jobs that an organization is interested in surveying in only one narrow category. There may be others that fall into a broader group. The point to all of this is that multiple decisions may be required before starting or participating in any survey activity. Much survey data is wasted and effort misspent by not identifying the target areas of interest ahead of time.

WHERE TO OBTAIN SURVEYS

After having decided on the market or markets we will participate in, we must obtain the necessary survey data. Again, there are multiple choices in doing this. We can conduct our own surveys, participate in exchange of survey data, hire or commission an outside group to do selected ones, or try a combination of the options listed.

The first step is to check what others in the area of industry you are in are doing. This, in essence, is a survey within a survey. It is usually a good benchmark on what you will find of use. If nothing else, it serves as a starting point.

Few organizations rely on a single survey. Most select broad surveys in their areas — e.g., steel companies are interested in the steel industry as well as heavy manufacturing in general. This provides the organization with a general overview of how their salary structure compares in the broadest sense.

There will always be additional survey information that will be needed. Using the same example of the steel company, what about selected specialists? For example, doctors, attorneys, programmers, etc., all are used in larger steel firms. They are not generic to the industry. Hence, their salary structure may vary from other jobs that are innate to that industry.

A survey system should be a series of steps or building blocks: first, seeing what other organizations are doing; then, determining what special jobs may need to be included; and, finally, determining any additional areas that management may wish to know about. These may be jobs that are presently not used, but will be due to the future acquisitions, mergers, or projected changes.

JOB STRUCTURING

The systems in this area are many in numbers. Any textbook on compensation will offer a series of options for grouping or structuring jobs. All of these will work to some degree. The question arises as to which one to select.

The answer, of course, varies by the organization. The point is to have a structure in place that will fairly pay or compensate based on market conditions. Secondly, the structure should be set up with benchmark positions that will allow a totally new job to be slotted in and paid according to its value. Figure 11-4 depicts such a structure.

There is a multitude of such systems to choose from. If one were to go to the library, one would find numerous books, papers, etc., dedicated to the topic. There also are many vendors and consultants available to aid in installing various job structure systems. This book can not begin to cover them. It can only point out their value and importance and, it is hoped, suggest or point out an approach to making a selection. Even if a system is in place, it might be wise to periodically reevaluate it.

Why would the system reevaluation be important? Compensation is one of the single most important factors in attracting and retaining qualified employees. When people are not paid adequately or feel that others doing jobs of the same value are paid too much, there is potential trouble. The employees are always measuring and evaluating, and the organization better have its house in order.

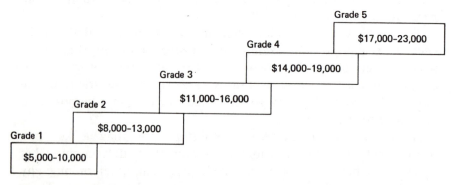

Fig. 11-4. Hypothetical job structuring system. (Jobs must be structured fairly in relation to their worth. The system must allow for new jobs to be added and paid for in relation to their value in comparison to others.)

How do you select a proper system? Again, and this is repetitious, but so important, take a look at others in similar organizations. Don't reinvent the wheel. Secondly, talk with some outside consultants familiar with your type of organization. A third party opinion can be a most valuable resource. They have probably reviewed many systems over the years and can point out some factors that would not be thought of.

The final step in the process is a review of the options and alternatives with management. Having established what other similar organizations are doing, then having the advice and suggestions from a third party, the stage is set. The decision on either the review of the existing system, or the setting up of a new one may not be easy, but the ingredients are there for use.

JOB DESCRIPTIONS

Job descriptions, if properly used, provide several benefits to an organization. First, they reduce to writing the various responsibilities, accountabilities, and relationships in a job. A sample job description is shown in Fig. 11-5. When the items listed are completely filled out, the actual length may be greater than the one-page example. It often takes two or more pages in the format shown to describe the job.

The process involved in the preparation of the job description is probably more important than the document itself. Figure 11-6 depicts some of the steps in preparing and using the job description. The real point is that it is far from a one-step operation. In some organizations, the steps shown may even be too few.

To begin with, someone has to analyze the job. In almost every case, this has to be someone with specific training in the area of job analysis. The incumbent in the job is usually a resource for information, but seldom trained in viewing the position analytically. This analysis may be done through an interview, a questionnaire covering the major points, a combination of interview and questionnaire, etc.

When the analyst feels that the job is fairly well understood, a series of drafts of the description normally is done. If the job is an existing one (rather than a new one), both the incumbent and at least one level of supervision are usually involved in the review and correction process. The levels and who reviews will vary from one organi-

Position Title: Personnel Systems Manager

Department: Personnel Systems

Responsibilities:

    1.

    2.   (Separate Paragraphs
               Listing the Tasks)
    3.

    4.

    Etc.

Scope: (Number of Supervised Budget Dollars)

Relationships: (List Who the Person Will Deal With)

Fig. 11-5. Job descriptions XYZ Corporation.

zation to another. Revisions will follow that then must be reviewed once more. This process should continue until everyone involved agrees that the description has captured the job in writing.

Fig. 11-6. Job description steps.

This is not the end of the process. The finalized draft becomes the working document for the job evaluation. Here, the value of the job is determined. The job is pegged in relation to other jobs, or slotted in with them. It is at this point that the rate range for the job is determined.

There are other systems to achieve this end. However, these steps are both logical and effective. They are time-consuming, but do provide a consistent approach for arriving at the value of a position. The job description provides the vehicle to accomplish this.

JOB SPECIFICATIONS

No discussion of job description is complete without touching on the concept of job specifications. (An exaggerated example is shown in Fig. 11-7.) This may give the connotation that they are at odds with each other; however, they really are not. It does point out that there is a problem in definition.

Job Specification	Job Description
1. Type 60-75 words a minute.	1. Provide rapid typing support.
2. Type 20 letters a day with 2% or less in error rate.	2. Accurately type letters as part of support.
3. File 50 documents a week with no errors.	3. Provide filing support unit.
4. Answer ten button telephone director with zero complaints regarding telephone skills	4. Answer phones in support of the unit.

Fig. 11-7 Job specifications versus job descriptions.

Frequently, a job description does only that — it describes the job or activity performed in general terms. It does not "specify" the skills and abilities that must be present in measurable form to actually do the job. The key to job specifications is the concept of being able to measure.

The single greatest pressure to go from job description to job specifications has come from the area of affirmative action. The government and courts have placed organizations in a defensive position. If charges of discrimination are levied, it becomes the organization's responsibility to disprove that they exist.

You cannot substantiate that the best qualified person was selected for the job if you can't measure the skills and qualifications required. This is putting a whole new dimension on how we look at jobs. There is now an intense effort to identify the measurable components that were often not pursued in the past.

Some positive tradeoffs have resulted from this. First, defining the specifications makes the vacancy filling much easier for employment (though more work for compensation). It is much easier to make a selection decision if you can verify the skills to do the job. The frequency of placing the wrong person in the job is greatly reduced.

The second, and possibly the most important, aspect of this movement toward job specifications is an effort to measure jobs in all categories and at all levels. For years we have had the ability to measure jobs in the manufacturing or production areas. We knew precisely the motions, efforts, number of turns, etc., that went into making "widgets" on the production line. Production control has been a well studied and documented area.

Today, many production jobs are being done by machine. Jobs are changing from production (blue collar) to service (white collar) type activities. These are areas that traditionally have not been subject to a great deal of measure.

With the switch comes the concept of possibly getting a handle on what managers and supervisors actually do. This is an area that has long been neglected. Not having measurement criteria has allowed poor supervisors and managers to continue in positions of responsibility undetected for many years — if not indefinitely. Obviously, the dollar costs to organizations from this area alone have been substantial.

Job specifications are not easy to establish. In areas such as supervision and management, new research has to be done to identify measurable items, activities, qualities, etc. However, as we change from a production- to a service-oriented society, this must be done anyway. To have value, something must be measurable, and the criteria must be identified and put into actual use.

WAGE AND SALARY INCREASE SYSTEMS

There are many types of salary increases. A few of these are shown in Fig. 11-8. They run the gamut from merit and promotion all the way to changes in the minimum wage.

Each organization is affected by a different set. For example, some may have very strict and detailed union agreements that spell out increases at specific times and in almost an automatic fashion. Within that organization, these set the precedent for increases for both union and non-union employees. Another organization may not have unions as a possible threat. In this case, no system is needed to track, follow, or implement union-related increases.

Another example might be a system to provide for changes in the minimum wage. Certain organizations in the United States fall under the law that requires that they pay no lower than a certain amount. This wage was constant for a number of years, but inflationary pressure has caused it to be changed more rapidly as purchasing power shifts.

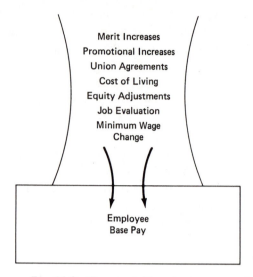

Merit Increases
Promotional Increases
Union Agreements
Cost of Living
Equity Adjustments
Job Evaluation
Minimum Wage
Change

Employee
Base Pay

Fig. 11-8. Wage and salary increases.

All organizations are not subject to minimum wage changes. Some, by the nature of their work, don't fall under the law. Others have their pay scales already set way above the minimum and aren't affected by a change in the legal rate. Thus, they are not in need of a system to track minimum wage changes.

The most prominent types of increases seem to be in the areas of merit, promotion, union agreement, and cost of living. Many organizations deny the existence of cost of living, and award increases (they say) "strictly on merit." This is very difficult, if not impossible, to do.

The cost of living change (which is basically up) is the basis for a major portion of the dollars in any increase system. (This is shown in Fig. 11-9.) Dollar increases or shrinkage to an organization's pool of money available to change wages and salaries is firmly based on the cost of living. Confronting this problem head-on may ward off other problems later.

A major portion of union agreements are arrived at based on what the negotiators involved feel will be needed to cover future price changes. The profitability of the organization involved is a bargaining chip, but not as significant as what both parties feel the economy will do with respect to inflation. The increased wage and salary amounts

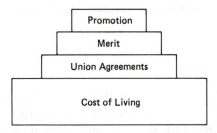

Fig. 11-9. Cost of living base. (Cost of living change, either up or down, is the basis for a major portion of the dollars in any increase system.)

are normally passed along to the consumer. Unions do, however, force recognition of some dollar factors such as merit and promotion, but in time of rapid inflation these become dwarfed by the cost of living factor.

Working our way up from the base in Fig. 11-9, we see that merit and promotion amounts are also rather small in comparison to the cost of living factor. The only time they are substantial as part of an organization's wage and salary pool is during the times of small inflation or deflation. If this economic situation is accompanied (as it usually is) by a recession, the wage and salary increase pool may be reduced to almost nothing.

During times of heavy inflation, the dollars made available for merits and promotions are also small if not nonexistent. Particularly in non-union areas, the dollars that cover cost of living are often masked as being for merit and promotion.

A system for management to fully identify and separate cost of living from merit dollars is vital. When an organization ceases to meet true merit and promotion requirements, trouble results.

The best performers are wise enough to realize that they are not moving forward even though a substantial percentage increase was given. They know if it covered present and future cost of living needs. When it has not, they become dissatisfied and move to another organization, where they have bargained for a substantial increase.

A decision to award cost of living disguised as merit or promotion is a frequently exercised management decision. However, we must be aware that the most valuable performers have their own system of analyzing their position. Management must have similar visibility into what constitutes merit and promotion dollars to remain competitive in the labor market.

MERIT AND PROMOTION

In setting up a wage and salary system, one of the first things any organization should do is define merit and promotion. The initial merit and promotion definition is important, since it can vary between organizations. This is not often recognized until one tries to define it for one's own area.

A merit increase may be viewed as additional pay for performing the same job in a better or more efficient manner. As noted before, if it is to be truly valuable to the employee, it must be in addition to the cost of living increase. This is frequently hard for management to adjust to in times of high inflation, since the dollar amounts seem so large. However, a merit increase must be larger than the employee's cost of living increase if we are truly rewarding increased performance and productivity.

The most difficult task is to define promotion. This can manifest itself in a change of title, salary grade, reporting level, etc. It is important that each organization think through and come to an internal agreement on measures or status changes that constitute promotion. These then should be reduced to writing and fully agreed to on all levels of management.

Why is it so important to separate merit from promotion? Primarily because it is a valued (by employees) part of the reward system that the organization has available to use. It is important that the most mileage be gained from it.

There are both economic and status factors involved in promotion. Most employees expect not only more money but some visible sign of increase in status with a promotion — e.g., a new title, a window office, an increased number of subordinates, his/her name on parking space. These status symbols may be even more important than the dollars in some organizations and to some individuals.

Some organizations are very effective in recognizing these tradeoffs. For example, financial institutions frequently use high-sounding titles in lieu of salary. Many people are willing to trade dollars for a Vice President or Senior Vice President title. One has but to look around at those with high-sounding positions with meager economic means to verify that this exists.

Often organizations trade on these status needs and increase their value. For example, if the organization says that only people at the senior management level have black chairs, then black chairs take on a value. People will aspire to having a black chair rather than a brown one, even though the seating comfort is identical. In this case, physical comfort doesn't equal psychological comfort.

This makes it even more important that we fully define the promotion system. In the case just cited, what happens if a lower level employee purchases a black chair and brings it into work? Does the organization fire him or her? Is the status symbol that has been created unrealistic?

We must take all the factors into account in defining promotion — dollars as well as status. They must be fully integrated to properly reward and motivate those involved, for that is what they are there for. At the same time, they must be logical and fair in both their worth and application.

TRACKING AND ANALYZING ORGANIZATION STRUCTURE CHANGES

An area that frequently falls under the compensation heading is that of organization analysis. Structure itself may dictate, at least partially, the pay rate involved. People in supervisory positions generally receive more pay than those in non-supervisory positions. One of the tests normally applied in job evaluation is whether or not the incumbent in a position supervises anyone as part of his/her duties.

Figure 11-10 shows how the same number of people in a work group can have different structures. Most of us know of organizations where there would be even a third level of supervision added. In this case, the one employee remaining would have several tiers of management above. This can be expensive to operate, as well as inefficient.

The major concern with any organization's system is flexibility. There is a tendency to try to set hard-and-fast rules. For example, the span of control of the number of people a person can directly supervise is often considered to be between three and five. We can all identify areas where this is not true. There are supervisors or managers who have only one or two people reporting to them, and others who

Organization Structure Impact

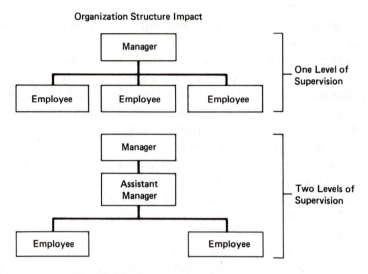

Fig. 11-10. Organization structure impact.

have sixteen or twenty. Both are able to handle the situations, and the operations function smoothly.

There is a tendency to make organization structure a mathematical formula. It would be so much easier to plug a number into an equation and get the proper structure. This is not the case; however, we can actually have some rather basic guidelines. Each organization change is a separate process that must be worked through with the end objective constantly kept in mind. There is no panacea that can be picked from the shelf and put into place. Each effort must be individualized to be effective.

The term "individualized" is the key to the problem. Firms organize around individuals. Responsibility for activity flows towards the managers who are strong in the ability to handle that particular activity. It flows away from those who are weak.

We organize around the specific strengths and weaknesses of people. Where this is not done, organization inefficiency will result. Limits of span of control, organizational depth, administrative support, supervisory/employee ratios, etc., are guidelines and *only* guidelines. If the personalities and abilities of the organization dictate a violation of these, we had better listen and look closely. Organizations and their structures are run by people in them and not by the guidelines!

RESPONSIBILITY FOR COMPENSATION SYSTEMS

The compensation activity is frequently housed under the personnel or human resource umbrella. This is one of the classic personnel or human resource functions that has traditionally been maintained.

Many people believe that personnel controls compensation policy. This is not correct. Compensation policy is controlled at the very top of any successful organization. The dollars involved are too great to delegate far from the apex of power.

The compensation area in personnel is responsible for monitoring and implementing the policies established by the president, chairman of the board, congress, etc. They by no stretch of the imagination set the policy. Understanding this concept is important, because even some in compensation do not fully realize their true role.

People often have to go to personnel to get increases approved. This often results in the feeling that personnel controls the dollars. It does, but only in very narrow ranges granted by higher authority. It would be almost impossible to find a personnel department or compensation division that could approve a 100% or 200% increase for employees. Few, if any, could decide to grant a double cost of living increase for all employees.

This perspective is important. The main role of personnel in this area is that of implementing and monitoring rather than decision-making. These activities lend themselves to a very logical systems approach in day-to-day activity. A control-oriented function must have tight systems in place.

12
BENEFITS SYSTEMS

A few years ago, a discussion of benefits systems would have been rel-
egated to a short paragraph or two in the chapter on compensation.
Now it demands a chapter on its own. What has changed to warrant
this?

A number of things have taken place to bring benefits to the forefront. First, let's take a look at where benefits stood several years ago.
As with most of personnel functions, it originated as a recordkeeping
function. Chances are a clerk was assigned to track the few people
who retired or the vacation days taken, or to process the occasional
medical claim after a large deductible had been met.

Unions probably did more than any group to bring the benefits
activity to its current importance. When wages became as high as it
seemed society would accept, then benefits became a realistic bargaining chip. These were passed along to the non-union workers, since
employers knew they would soon unionize if they didn't receive equal
treatment.

Benefits often receive positive tax treatment. In many instances,
they are not taxed. As people moved into higher tax brackets, and
as taxes increased in amount and type, benefits grew in value. To a
larger segment of the population, a dollar in benefits was worth much
more. As this became apparent, the demand for increased benefits
began to rise at all levels in the organization.

Concern over the abuse by organizations administering the benefits
has also increased. This has resulted in additional legislative controls.
One of the most prominent of these is ERISA, which was discussed
earlier. Looking toward the future, we can anticipate more legislation

in the area of control, since the size of benefit packages and their dollar value are on the increase.

The cost of benefits to the organizations involved grows annually. Medical costs alone, which used to be minor, are now staggering. The benefit dollar as a percentage of the payroll is ever increasing. It won't be long before the dollars spent on benefits will be the same or more than those spent on payroll.

BENEFITS FUNCTIONS

A partial list of benefits functions is given in Fig. 12-1. This list targets the major benefits functions that are in use at this time. Each of these, in turn, requires a system or systems to assure proper implementation, administration, and use.

Benefits administration is one of the first items on the list. With the growth of both the size and dollars involved in benefits, it is important that an adequate administrative system be in place. There are many items that must have proper coordination for the activity to function properly.

Not the least of these is a system to track new legislation and the interpretation of existing laws. These are continually changing, and anyone not constantly monitoring this activity will rapidly fall behind. The changes that these create require a flexible body of policy and procedure guides for the line or operating activities. (This is shown in Fig. 12-2.)

The medical or health areas shown, as noted earlier, are among the most costly benefits systems. Originally, coverage was provided for

Benefits Administration
Medical/Health
Disability
Life Insurance
Pension/Retirement
Special Benefits
Executive Perquisites

Fig. 12-1. Benefit functions.

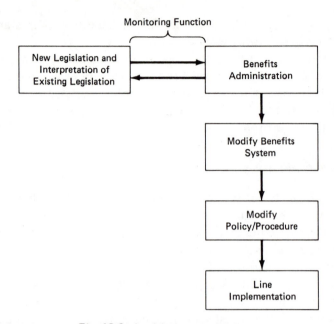

Fig. 12-2. Legislative monitoring.

the workers, then the addition was made to add dependents. In some instances, there is a partial payment by the employee for these coverages, but the trend in the United States is toward the organization making total payments for all coverage through major medical.

More recently, medical insurance coverage has been broadened. Many organizations have added such items as dental care, drugs, psychiatric care, and vision (eye) care to the policy. These alone, even without the increase in medical charges, greatly add to what an organization must pay.

The systems to support the medical or health care area are substantial. Claims processing is extremely complex and time-consuming. Many organizations have gone to outside services to aid in their processing, or are using rather sophisticated computer systems. The days when a clerk with a small amount of training could handle the processing are over for an organization of any size.

Disability insurance is another area of increased costs. This extends from the salary continuation or sick leave through more lengthy short-term disability and long-term disability. This category of disability was at one time left to the discretion of the supervisor or manager involved. In the case of an extremely good worker, the pay might be continued on an exception basis.

With the concerns that have risen over discrimination, equal treatment of employees, etc., this has been formalized. Most organizations have formulas spelling out the specific coverage that is available to employees. The system is usually predicated on such factors as whether the employee is hourly or salaried and his/her length of service.

Costs have increased as items such a pregnancy and mental disorders have been included. Psychiatric disabilities are often hard to measure. As the complexity of society and everyday living has compounded problems, we see a rise in costly mental disabilities. This is not apt to abate in the near future. In fact, as society continues to become more complex and as activities speed up, we will see increased costs in this area.

Life insurance is another area that needs system support. The cost has not been rising as dramatically as in other areas. However, the breadth and types of insurance in this area has been increasing. Insurance might include group life insurance, dependent group life insurance, travel accident insurance, and key "man" insurance. The system must be responsive to handling the increased options that are often made available to organizations and their employees.

Another function that now requires a rather sophisticated tracking system is that of pension and retirement benefits. Many new requirements of reporting, vesting, etc., have been brought into play by ERISA. The complexity is so great that many organizations find it necessary to go to outside sources for guidance and assistance.

The area of pension and retirement is also much broader than the first glance would indicate. There are many things in this category other than just pension benefits. For example, thrift plans, profit sharing plans, pension death benefits to survivors, and deferred compensation coverage all fall under this umbrella.

Many people don't view profit sharing and thrift plans as part of a pension benefit. However, in concept, most are geared to supplement other retirement income. This has led to their inclusion in the ERISA area of control

Special benefits is a growing area that may require system support at varying levels. Included in this area are such diverse items as group legal coverage, tuition reimbursement, locating jobs for spouses, vacations and holidays, and group auto insurance. These all have the potential to split out into individual categories of their own.

Executive perquisites have been with us for a long time. Some include them with benefits, and others treat them as a separate item. They are much sought after, and as any executive recruiter will note, often are a major consideration in accepting or rejecting a job offer. They provide the executive with additional items of material value that often are not taxable to him or her. Executive perquisites are broad in range and include a company car, company credit cards, use of corporate planes, executive dining rooms, first class travel, choice of office furnishings, financial planning, and club memberships. The list is actually limited only to one's imagination.

Outside of the tax advantage is the status implication. After a certain level of income is achieved or wealth accumulated, the status factor plays an even greater part. Having access to a corporate jet or being able to travel first class on commercial flights indicates that one is held in high value by the organization involved.

There is a clear message to peers, subordinates, and contemporaries in the individual's profession that he or she is highly valued. Executive perquisites are often more visible than salary dollars, which are frequently kept confidential. Perquisites are often a visible badge of recognition of having arrived at a certain level of success.

HIDDEN PAYROLL IMPACT

Both classical benefits and perquisites cost money. Someone has to pay for the dramatically increasing medical/dental costs. The prices of company cars and commercial transportation are rising very rapidly. The organization is the one meeting these increases. Those organizations that are able to will pass them along to their customers wherever possible.

Even if no new benefits or perquisites are added, these costs are going to continue to go up. Since they are frequently in the commercial area, their costs may go up much faster than the wages paid to employees. Prices of goods and services in time of inflation can outpace the increases in wages and salaries.

Most organizations can limit additions of new benefits or perquisites, but can do little about those already available. Reducing medical coverage, cutting pension support, or taking away a company car are not viable options. Doing these things are like asking for people to resign. Even if it is shown to employees that such measures are economic necessities for the organization, the chances of passive acceptance are small. Most people today feel it is the responsibility of the organization both to provide and maintain these items. Those organizations that do not make these provisions soon find themselves in a difficult competitive situation in the labor market.

As discussed earlier, benefits are costing organizations more money, and it is quite possible that this amount will soon meet or exceed the dollars paid as salary. The marketplace will force this to occur. Figure 12-3 shows the human resource market. Resources will flow to those offering a greater range of perquisites and benefits. People in today's labor market are sophisticated and are aware of the value these have. Organizations that feel they can save money in this area will quickly lose any competitive advantage in obtaining and retaining human resources.

INTERNAL OR EXTERNAL SYSTEMS

To a large extent, benefit systems have probably achieved a greater level of sophistication than many personnel systems, the reason being that they have had a great deal of outside assistance and role models

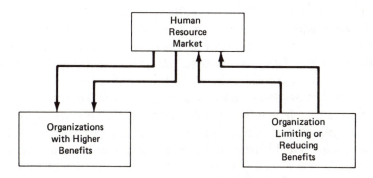

Fig. 12-3. Human resource market.

to either purchase or pattern after. Who are these models? The insurance companies.

Many of the benefits offered are of the insurance variety — e.g., medical, dental, life, disability. Sophisticated insurance companies have been around for a greater length of time than sophisticated personnel departments. Many insurance companies have been in the forefront of the development of actuarial tables, the use of management science and computers, etc. Hence, there is a substantial number of systems and techniques developed in the area.

This provides the benefits activity of an organization with a wide array of time-tested options. Other areas of personnel certainly have make or buy options, as we discussed earlier, but possibly not with the proven breadth and depth that those in benefits have. It is fairly easy to find other organizations that have been operating for years with a purchased, leased, or rental benefit system or systems. This in itself provides a base for review and consideration.

Those in benefits have many options on how they may wish to administer a given program. For example, take the medical program. This can range all the way from a self-administered program with internal claims processing, to one where the entire package is turned over to an outside broker or company. It can be reduced to where all the organization provides is a periodic list of eligible employees and the check for providing the service.

The same thing just noted applies to the other benefits functions. There are very sophisticated and experienced services available to handle all aspects of the benefits activity. There are definitely cost tradeoffs, and these must be weighed as with any other business decision. In essence, the entire benefits activity could be run with little more than a small administrative staff that actually was on the organization's payroll. The major portion of the activity can be subcontracted out. There is a cost to doing this, but due to economics of scale it may be less than the cost of doing it in-house.

The options available to do this exist to some degree in other personnel areas, such as training and development. Outside firms can be found to put on the various programs the organization may require. It does seem that, in benefits, there is both a stronger precedent for using outside services and a greater depth and breadth of these avail-

able.   There are some very large old line corporations in business that
have been handling organization's benefits' needs successfully over extended periods of time.   This record is worthy of consideration.

PENSION AND RETIREMENT SYSTEMS CONCERNS

In an earlier chapter discussing the legal aspects of personnel, the concept of ERISA (Employee Retirement Income Security Act) was discussed.   Its essence is to ensure that those participating in a pension
plan found it available when retirement came.   It is a United States
law aimed at protecting the employee's retirement.

There has been a lot of concern by firms large and small regarding
both the interpretation and implementation of ERISA.   Many smaller
organizations have been so confused that they have abandoned the
idea of offering a retirement plan.   The work, concern and potential
liability have proven too overwhelming.

This is one area in which most organizations are forced to go to an
outside (or buy) decision.   A personnel organization should not try to
"go it alone" in either setting up a pension/retirement system or administering an existing one.   The problems and complexities are too
great.   All organizations need the assistance of an outside consultant
(attorney, CPA firm, ERISA consultant, etc.) on this topic.   It will
probably be many years before the interpretation process of the law
is completed, and before sufficient in-house expertise will reside within
personnel to totally depend on internal resources.

CAFETERIA BENEFITS SYSTEMS

The concept of cafeteria benefits is becoming popular.   This basically
means that the employee selects the benefits package that best fits
his or her needs.   Frequently, regardless of the popularity of the concept, benefits packages are blanket in nature rather than cafeteria style.
There is one medical/dental plan, one life insurance policy, one disability plan, etc., which applies to everyone.

As we know, everyone is not the same.   People have varied benefits
desires and requirements.   These not only vary by individual, but vary
for the same individual over time.   In fact, there are many factors in-

volved in what types of benefits a person needs and/or desires (Fig. 12-4 depicts this).

An organization is not necessarily getting "full mileage" or even "partial mileage" out of its benefits plan if it is not meeting employee needs. It may be spending millions of dollars and actually creating dissatisfaction among the staff.

For example, an extensive pension/retirement plan may have little value to employees in the twenty and thirty year age range. Even though it may be one of the finest plans in the world, it has little or no impact on an age group that isn't presently concerned with pension/retirement. If the dollars are put into this category at the expense of other categories that the younger age group is interested in, the effect may be negative.

This can be a crucial factor in recruiting and retaining people. What labor market are we trying to tap? Which employees do we want most to retain? Do our benefits programs meet these needs? Are all groups satisfied with the benefits package?

Chances are that with a blanket benefit program that is identical for everyone, the answers to these questions are not always positive. The cafeteria approach may provide a system, or a set of systems, that reverses this and allows a more positive return on the benefits dollars being spent. The employees choose the portions they need. The older employees may opt for greater pension/retirement, while younger employees may select more extensive dependent medical coverage.

One of the major problems is setting up a system to administer this activity. Different benefits have different price tags. Employees must

Benefits Requirements	Yes	No
1. Varies by individual interest?	X	
2. Varies over time (age)?	X	
3. Varies by marital status?	X	
4. Varies by family size?	X	
5. Varies by financial condition?	X	
Etc.		

Fig. 12-4. Individual benefit requirements.

be given a dollar limit in their selection process, and this must be monitored and controlled. Then questions arise, such as what if one benefit starts to rise dramatically in price? Does the employee make a new selection to see that he or she stays under the limit, or make up the difference by personal payment? At the other extreme, what about employees who don't use all of their benefit allowance? The system has to be designed to handle these situations.

Many organizations that have a blanket benefit program can offer some additional cafeteria benefits to employees at no cost to the organization, but at reduced cost to the employee. The group rates available to organizations make this an attractive option. For example, dependent life insurance can be arranged for employees at costs substantially below what they would have to pay as individuals. The same group rate reduction can be found on many benefits, and the employee profits by having the option to purchase these at the organization's group rate discount. There is *no* cost to the organization, with the exception of making the announcement of availability. In some cases, the employer may incur some nominal charges for forms and processing if a payroll deduction is involved; however, these are usually small.

The major problem that can result in doing this is past precedent on who pays for employee benefits. If the organization has picked up the entire tab in the past, employees may resent having to pay for a new benefit even at reduced rates. They are conditioned to the employer paying. Also, where a union is involved, the payment may become an item for negotiation. Thus, the organization may be forced to pay the amount for the employees, if not initially, then during a future bargaining session.

SECURITY SYSTEM

Personnel information is traditionally considered confidential, and is treated accordingly. Benefits is an area of ever greater concern because of the nature of the information involved. Dollars are spent, claims are made, audits must occur, etc. Information flows into benefits and must be treated confidentally; however, there are substantial requirements for outside dissemination just to get the daily job accomplished.

Figure 12-5 shows what we are confronted with. Information flows into benefits through normal personnel channels. In other areas of personnel, most data is retained internally or shared with management on a "need to know basis." In benefits, this is different because of the myriad of people, outside groups, etc., that must be dealt with.

This becomes a more serious problem as greater emphasis is placed on confidentiality. Unless totally self-insured, there will be (usually several) insurance carriers involved. In addition, various government agencies become involved in certain injury claims. The need to release personal information to outside organizations does not stop with employees, but extends often to their dependents, who are frequently involved in various insurance coverages.

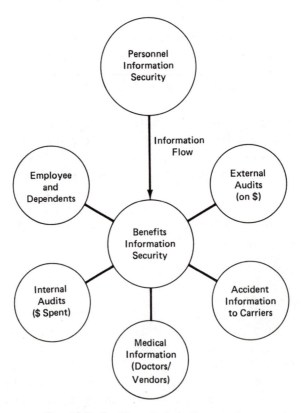

Fig. 12-5. Problems in benefits security.

Outside insurance carriers are very careful in restricting access to information they receive. Their security measures are usually extensive, since their business depends on them. In fact, they can be a source for a benefits department to turn to for guidance in setting up its own security.

The problem that benefits departments are confronted with is the large number of people who require access, not the fact that these sources are security problems. It is just that as we increase numbers having access, the greater is the possibility that some form of leak may occur.

Along with the concern to maintain confidentiality of personnel benefits data comes certain legal responsibilities to which benefits must adhere. These entail such steps as obtaining written permission to release data from the employees, and often involve not only permission to release employee data, but information on dependents as well.

An organization would be well advised to have an outside expert, possibly from one of its carriers, periodically review compliance in this area. The term "periodically" should be stressed, since laws and requirements in this area frequently change. When they do change, the trend is to place more responsibility and additional compliance requirements on the organization. It would be very easy to be in violation of the law in this area and not even be aware of it.

FUTURE OF BENEFITS

If there is any organization in the personnel area that is truly in an expansion phase, it is benefits. Projections do not indicate any slackening of the continued expansion. Benefits seems to be an area of continued legislative attention. Every law or legislative control just increases the work for an organization. This, in turn, requires expansion of the activity that supports this compliance.

This has resulted in a great deal of labor-intensive activity. In many firms, the number of people in the benefits area is now greater than in any other department or division in personnel. Both now and in the future, we see greater use of automation in benefits to try to stem the need for increases in costly labor.

Automation is easily marketed where direct cost savings are readily available. In large companies, there is no longer any question that immediate savings are available by automating the benefits activity. Right now, some of the most sophisticated computer systems used in administrative areas are found in benefits. It appears that in the future we will see the latest automated system applied in this area, due to the large and immediate cost savings available. This will spill over and give all of personnel a higher priority for access to the latest and most efficient advances in automation, which in itself has very positive ramifications for everyone in the personnel field.

13
EMPLOYEE RELATIONS
AND RESEARCH SYSTEMS

People working together in any group have problems, concerns, needs, desires, ambitions, etc., because they are human. These factors exist at all levels and in multiple variations. Day-to-day operations do not run smoothly, and conflicts can, and do, result.

When these problems affect the organization's ability to perform its mission or function, someone has to act as the mediator. Where people- or personnel-type concerns are involved, this may fall to someone in the employee relations area. This "someone" frequently represents both management and the employee. The aim is to resolve any conflict in the best interests of everyone involved.

This is not a series of functions that strictly applies to dealing with people. In fact, there are many behind-the-scene non-people, mechanical activities that must be accomplished to assure that fairness and equity are parts of the results. These include, but aren't limited to, such things as writing and maintaining policies and procedures, surveys, and staff planning.

Some feel that the research activities and systems are separate from those of employee relations. There definitely is a trend in this direction. Several large organizations show personnel research as a separate box on the organization chart. There is no question that personnel research is a separate and distinct body of knowledge in the personnel area and that it may be spun off as a separate entity. However, it is often maintained as a support function attached to one of the classical personnel activities — usually employee relations.

EMPLOYEE RELATIONS AND RESEARCH FUNCTIONS

An administrative system is one of the first shown in Fig. 13-1. Any major area or body of activity needs to have a focus of control. Due to the complexity and wide range of impact of the systems in the employee relations and research area, this is particularly true. This area — administration — allows for systems to ensure proper communication and policy application. Without some central control, multiple interpretations and applications will exist.

Policy and procedure systems are shown next. No single set of systems is so important to a smooth and well run personnel department. When they do not exist, the organization is wide open to all types of grievance, strikes, lawsuits, etc.

Without personnel policies and procedures, there is no consistency or uniformity. Each supervisor/manager must develop his or her own. This can create a wide range of problems. For example, one supervisor may award an employee severance pay at termination, while another does not. One supervisor may give three warnings to an errant employee before discharging him/her. A second may give one warning, and a third may summarily discharge an employee for the same offense. This makes an organization a target for grievances and lawsuits of all types.

Administration
Policies and Procedures
Employee Communication and Counseling
Union or Union Prevention
Government Agencies and Special Interest Groups
Exit Interviewing
Affirmative Action Program
Attitude Surveys
Hiring and Testing Criteria
Staff Planning

Fig. 13-1. Employee relations and research functions.

A personnel department without clearly defined policies and pro-cedures is ripe for one emergency after another. Those that spend most of their time "fighting fires" usually do so because of the lack of clearly defined policies and procedures. They not only have to be in existence, but supervision must be aware of them. Ideally, periodic training sessions should be conducted to answer questions and update those involved. The time spent in doing this actually saves time later on, since guidelines poorly administered always lead to problems.

Employee communications systems cover a wide range of activities. In a small organization, this may be limited to those in personnel having an "open door," or frequently circulating and individually talking with employees. In large organizations, this may entail having periodic surveys, field representatives, special confidential phone lines where employees can call anonymously with questions, etc.

Management must be aware of how the employees think and feel regarding all aspects of their jobs. When communications break down, problems of all types result. No organization can function effectively with even a few disgruntled staff members. It is like any other disease — it tends to spread and infest the entire organization.

If a union exists in an organization, fairly sophisticated systems must be set up to deal with it. There are negotiations to handle, con-tracts to administer, formal grievance procedures, etc. Even where a union does not exist, there is always the potential that one will come into existence. If management does not want one, then selected pre-ventive systems must be set up and maintained. It should always be kept in mind that the existence of unions has done much to enhance the need for a strong and well-managed personnel department. This holds true regardless of whether a union exists or not; *potential* for one is always in existence.

More and more, we are seeing systems set up in personnel to deal with government agencies and special interest groups. The larger the organization and the greater its visibility, the more time that must be spent in responding to government-required surveys, meeting with consumer or human rights groups, and so on.

Few organizations are isolated or insulated from the outside world in today's society. Systems must be set up to deal with these outside concerns or they may become major personnel problems. Just recog-nizing their existence is not sufficient. They must be identified, since they vary by organization, and a system or systems must be set up to deal with them.

Exit interviewing is another system that can provide valuable information. Why turnover is existing can be significant. If large numbers are leaving because of salary, we may no longer be competitive. However, if the complaints are about certain supervisors, increasing salaries would not be the answer. The exit interview gives us some insight into why people are leaving.

Almost everyone has to work. No one leaves an organization voluntarily if he or she is happy, or as happy as it is imagined that the new organization will make him/her. We may want to have two or more systems for exit interviewing: one to talk to people at the time they leave, and a follow-up questionnaire to their homes after they have been gone for a month or more.

The two-pronged system is often quite effective. When people are exiting an organization, they may be reluctant to tell the real reason (unless they are angry) until they are settled in their new position. The questionnaire sent out at a later date catches these. Those who are really angry or upset may provide the information at the first interview. Combining the two methods gives the organization both a "safety valve" and an opportunity to cross-check the real reasons people are leaving.

The function and related sets of systems for affirmative action is shown here as part of employee relations and research. This can vary from organization to organization. In some, it will be shown reporting directly to the president or chief operating officer. The pattern has the function most often in the personnel department and as part of the employee relations activity. It is shown here in that context.

Affirmative action's very dynamic and changing nature, again, requires significant systems flexibility. Each new court decision can have broad ramifications. Placing it close to the personnel research aspect of the operation adds to the flexibility in being able to provide analytical support.

Attitude surveys can show management what employees feel about a wide range of topics. The standard approach to doing this is via survey forms. There is a danger in asking people's opinions. Once you have asked, they expect both feedback on the survey and some actions taken to resolve the problems. Management may not be in a position, or may not want, to do either.

For example, a survey is conducted to review existing attitudes regarding salaries and benefits. The results show that the employees feel their salaries are too low, and the company's dental plan is terrible. Now, management has been informed of the problems, and the employees expect corrective action. Depending on the size of the organization, raising salaries and upgrading the dental plan could cost millions of dollars. The anticipated revenues may not be sufficient to cover this.

Many organizations feel that through proper communication they can have the benefits of the survey information, and improve overall employee relations. In the case just cited, the employees would have to be informed of the results and the problems with solving the situation due to the adverse profit picture of the company. This, if handled properly, could provide a workable temporary solution. However, when profits improve, the issue will have to be confronted again.

Hiring and testing criteria is another area of both current interest and heavy activity. A large portion of this has stemmed from various legal concerns raised due to affirmative action decisions. All aspects of hiring — including the application, interview process, and testing — must meet rather stringent tests to ensure that discriminatory practices do not exist. Systems must be set up to verify this compliance and provide tracking for audit purposes.

Many organizations are also starting to focus on the benefits they receive from proper selection procedures. If they truly match the proper person with the proper job, they avoid future employee relations problems as well as the costs of replacement when turnover occurs. It is becoming more difficult to release people without substantial justification. Consequently, it is becoming increasingly important that we place the right people in the proper jobs to begin with.

Staff planning is another aspect that must be handled through a series of properly positioned systems. Organizations grow and expand, as well as shrink and contract as they go through various phases of an organizational life cycle. Employees are always concerned and disturbed by any change, since it creates an unknown in the environment. It is important to identify changes well in advance. By doing so, the organization can ensure proper development and placement of resources, and the employees can be involved in the decision-making process. This helps in reducing the unrest and concern that is normally experienced during times of change.

IMPORTANCE OF STATISTICAL DATA

Statistical data is important in performing the employee relations function, and not just in support of the research aspect. The impact of this is shown in Fig. 13-2. First, the issue of servicing the needs of management and the organization are identified as part of the research activity.

Many people think of statistical data as being purely something of use and interest for management. To a certain degree, this is correct, since management has control over the sources and compilation of such data. However, if properly administered and used, it can be of major benefit to the employees.

For example, we previously discussed the use of employee attitude surveys, and how such information, if acted upon, can eliminate complaints. Another area is maintaining statistical visibility in the affirmative action mix. Not only knowing what it is, but taking action to ensure a proper balance, can prevent suits and problems in this area.

The other area noted under employee relations is to be in a position to factually answer employee questions. What new openings are anticipated? Is there room for growth? For an unhappy employee, a transfer out of the present area may be just the tonic being sought. Here, we see the benefits of statistics, not just for management, but directly for the employees.

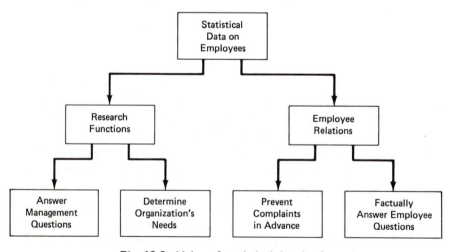

Fig. 13-2. Value of statistical data banks.

OPEN DOOR POLICY

We all feel frustrated and helpless at times. Employees, as well as supervisors, experience these feelings. They are natural danger signals that can lead to problems in an organization if not handled properly. The personnel department, and specifically employee relations, is often designated as the safety valve.

Keeping communication channels open in a wide variety of ways is of major importance. It will take more than one system to do this, one reason being that everyone is not comfortable with the same system. Some want to read about change in the house organ, or in a special newsletter; others want a confidential phone line to call, or a face-to-face individual meeting.

Again, the system must have flexibility. The large selection of items is shown in Fig. 13-3. Organizations will vary the mix of these over time. Circumstances and operations are ever-changing. These will be most heavily used during times of major change to the organization, since large numbers of people are concerned when major change is occurring.

Times of both good and bad occurrences are when the communications channels are needed the most. Too often, we feel that we need to use the communications systems to explain the impact of something bad — such as layoffs due to reduction in orders or loss of a contract.

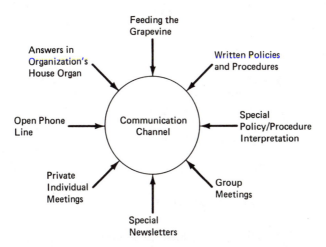

Fig. 13-3. Need for multiple communications systems.

In actuality, there is often as much concern and unrest when something good is occurring.

When something bad happens, employees expect to be affected in a negative way (e.g., layoffs). When something good is happening to the organization, they expect to share in some of this. Questions of the positive things that may occur need to be addressed. Will there be added raises and bonuses? What about the opportunity for overtime pay? (This could be negative if leisure has a high value to the individual.) What about promotions? What about training? New cafeteria facilities?

TOOLS FOR MANAGERS

Though personnel through its employee relations and research function should be available to answer employee questions, supervision at all levels plays a key role. Figure 13-4 shows this role. It is natural, since the first line of contact with the employee is the manager or supervisor. Part of personnel's job is to maintain open channels of communication.

In reality, the role of personnel or employee relations is, and should be, secondary to that of management. One of the major functions of management is to funnel information both vertically (to supervisors

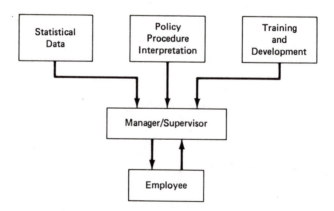

Fig. 13-4. Managerial tools.

and subordinates) and horizontally (to peers). Employee relations is, or should be, a staff position providing support for the managers.

For example, systems need to be established by employee relations to support management's needs, as noted in Fig. 13-4. Statistical data needs to be identified and provided to management in a readily usable form. Information such as salary ranges, minority statistics, staff growth, exempt/non-exempt ratios, and department counts is useful in responding to employee inquiries. Any statistics available from the manpower or staff planning area are usually particularly useful. Here might be included items such as projected staff growth, new job opportunities, new locations that will be opened, and trends in employment.

Any item that affects an employee's job will definitely be of concern to him/her. Many organizations have found it of value to supply managers with a statistical manual of significant information. This can be of extensive value in large organizations, where statistical information is not always readily available. This may aid in heading off both the feeling of being lost in the structure, as well as the distribution of erroneous or conflicting information.

Management will constantly need to be supplied with information on new or revised policies and procedures. Coupled with this is the corresponding interpretations that must be made. Employee relations must ensure that proper counsel and guidance are available in this area. It is all too easy to have varied and sometimes conflicting application of the same policy and procedure. Misinterpretation can easily occur if proper support and clarity are not available.

These needs lead us to the third item noted in the figure: a need for training and development of managers in proper communication. The larger the organization, the more important such a system becomes. The better the training in the use of statistical systems, the more effective and consistent will be their use.

Obviously, there is a gap that management cannot fill. This occurs when there has been a breach or disagreement between the manager and the subordinate. Where this exists, the manager must rely on personnel (employee relations). It is at this point that employee relations should become directly involved with the employee, and with the manager separately. In this secondary or back-up role, employee relations is most effective and useful to everyone involved. (This relationship is shown in Fig. 13-5.)

PERSONNEL RECORDS

When the line relationship has deteriorated and the employee wants to talk to a third party (employee relations), this third party needs a reference point. In a small organization, the need for such a reference point may not be as critical, since most people know one another. However, it is not uncommon for the personnel in a small organization's employee relations function to ask for the personnel record (sometimes called personnel file, personnel folder, etc.).

In a large organization, the personnel record or file is vital in employee relations counseling. It provides a picture of the employee's background and work history. If used properly, the employee relations specialist can have at least a basic idea of the type of individual he or she will be dealing with, and if similar past problems or complaints have existed.

This requires a rather sophisticated system or systems for record-keeping, which increases as the size of the organization changes. One of the first concerns is a determination of what material will be maintained on employees. This can range from the initial resume, employment applications, etc., through the most current status change (e.g., change in department number, rate increase, etc.). These rec-

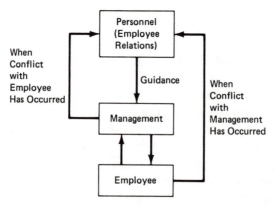

Fig. 13-5. Employee relations secondary or back-up position.

ords may also contain performance evaluations, formal counseling sessions, training courses taken, letters of commendation, and award certificates.

The use of automation in this area is still somewhat limited. We are frequently dealing with documents rather than specific data elements. Though there may be certain standard documentation, such as an employment application or copies of the organization's status change forms, other, non-standard documents may vary by individual. For example, school certificates, resumes, and letters of commendation may vary significantly depending on their source.

There have been some attempts at the use of automated microfilm systems to capture, store, and retrieve personnel records. The display capability for some of the more recent computers also provides possibilities for furthering the automated aspects. However, most personnel records, even in large, sophisticated organizations, are maintained in manila folders or the like. Record clerks still manually file and retrieve data as requested.

There is obviously a large interest in automating records. At least a portion in any large organization is on the personnel computer file. However, few systems have totally done away with the manila folders that tend to exist in any organization. It would appear that technically this step is feasible, but from a cost point of view the manual portion of the system is still viable.

LEGAL ASPECTS OF RECORDS SYSTEMS

As was discussed earlier, personnel has been affected in the United States by a myriad of laws and regulations. The recordkeeping areas have not escaped this. Not only do these laws cover the types of information that may or may not be maintained, but the questions of access by those on whom they are kept.

One of the fears regarding the maintaining of records is privacy. Everyone has certain things they would not like indiscriminately revealed. The reasons for this are many and varied. Also of concern is that files may be established that are in error. The incorrect file may be personally damaging.

Most people have experienced an erroneous billing that must be straightened out. The frustration level increases if a computer is involved. Frequently, even after we are assured corrective action, the error continues to cause problems and to recur. It often takes several concerted efforts before the situation is resolved. This just fuels the fear and concerns about organizational recordkeeping.

Employees now must be able to review the files maintained on them. In the past, a supervisor could slip a derogatory note in the personnel record without concern that the employee would ever know. This could haunt the employee for years — causing management to hold back raises and promotions, to subject the individual to layoff in times of a downturn, etc. What if the information was not correct? What if the supervisor had a personal grudge? What if the supervisor feared that the employee was a threat to his/her own position? All of these things happen daily in all organizations.

The only protection is to mandate that the employee has the right to review his or her own file. This prevents erroneous or unsubstantiated information from entering the file, and allows for correction when it does. (This is shown in Fig. 13-6.) Some feel this limits the ability to keep records; however, it goes far in ensuring the quality and fairness of the system. In the long run, this may be the most important factor.

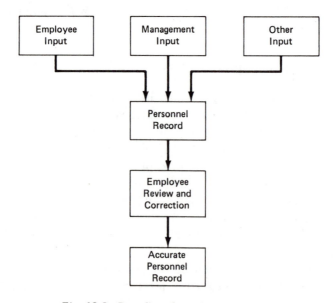

Fig. 13-6. Benefits of employee review.

DATING OF EMPLOYEE INFORMATION

The information that was collected on employees used to stretch over an entire lifetime or work history period. For example, job applications used to ask that a person detail his/her work history all the way back to a first job. This entailed giving a great deal of time to research and maintaining historical data. In some cases, organizations would reference-check all of the employers shown. This required a rather extensive system for employers to request information and respond to others.

Today, we have minimized some of the history that is requested of an employee. We often do not ask for more than five years of work history. Time has accelerated the obsolescence. What someone did ten or twenty years ago probably does not have the value in assessing performing a present task that it once might have. With changing technology, activities not performed in a recent time period soon become outdated. A person must remain current in his/her field to have value. In some cases, but not all, this has reduced the need for extensive historical systems.

UNION IMPACT

Earlier, we discussed the fact that unions have added to the power of personnel. A strike can close an organization down and negotiations can result in increased expenses of millions of dollars. Those who deal with unions through negotiations and day-to-day contract interpretations have power.

It was also pointed out that dealing with the unions may be a function of employee relations, a separate entity within personnel, or an independent but closely allied industrial relations department. Regardless, the impact of a union in an organization is significant to employee relations.

Items can be spelled out in the contract, such as steps for terminating employees, layoff procedures during slack periods, vacation periods, and grievance and counseling steps. This can reduce the flexibility an employee relations activity may have in establishing policy and procedures, since it becomes an item in the bargaining process.

Those items affecting employee relations identified in a union contract must have a system designed to make sure they are carried out.

For example, let us assume that layoffs due to lack of work are to be carried out in seniority order with the employees being given two weeks' advance notice. Several systems must be set up just to accomplish this. First, one must be designed to maintain a seniority listing so we know who is affected. Second, a system has to be set up to notify the employees who will be laid off, assuring proper implementation of the two weeks.

This clause in the contract does not stop here as far as its impact on the organization's systems. Figure 13-7 points out a portion of the impact this will have. The seniority system will need support systems to track such things as new hires and terminations. Even the terms "hire" and "termination" may require redefinition, because in this example they affect just the seniority list and not the entire organization. If a person were promoted to a supervisory position, he or she might leave the union, thus leaving the seniority list, without having terminated from the company.

The two weeks notice system must trigger a series of other actions or systems. What about payments for unused vacation, calculation

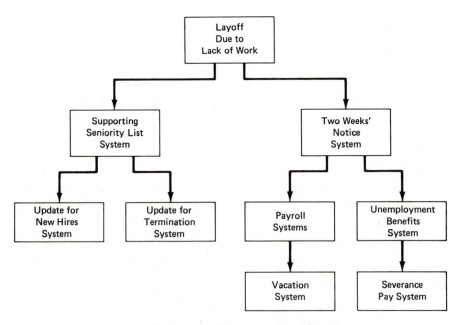

Fig. 13-7. Systems to support systems.

of severance, etc.? By the same token, what about unemployment benefits — if any? How are the employees advised of what exists, and guided through any sign-up procedures?

Systems beget systems. Too frequently, the only costs identified by an organization are the direct impact of salary increases and new benefits programs being considered during negotiations. They argue over pennies and make changes that can cost millions when all the system's revisions are completed.

This is not by design, but more probably due to the lack of information. Few organizations realize the existence and complexity of their systems, let alone having adequate cost figures. In reality, it could be less costly to give a nickel an hour raise, rather than modify the seniority clause and change the severance policy system. The need is to realize that system costs exist, and to at least estimate their impact even if hard dollar figures are not available.

14
THE FUTURE OF PERSONNEL SYSTEMS

The philosophy that states that what is done today determines what tomorrow will be certainly applies here. Those organizations that are actively recognizing the importance of personnel systems will have an advantage. Recognizing and starting to do something about them will dictate tomorrow's system structure.

No major system is developed and put into place overnight. Even if one were to purchase a system, it would take a certain amount of advance planning and study. Cost comparisons must be made, vendors researched, and references checked. Deciding which personnel system best fits the organization in question is not a simple task but a very complex one, if it is done right.

COMPUTER COSTS AND AVAILABILITY

There is a direct relationship to the costs and availability problem of computers and the use of them in personnel. Figure 14-1 depicts this relationship. Certain aspects were discussed in an earlier chapter. It was pointed out that line- or income-producing units tended to have a higher priority than administrative areas, which included personnel.

There have been changes in both the view of personnel and the costs and availability of computer services. This projects very positively into the future. First, the groundwork has been set for a change in how personnel is viewed. Frequently, the term "human resources" is applied, replacing the older "personnel" concept.

When employees are viewed as a resource rather than as an expense item, the picture starts to change. Time and dollars are more available

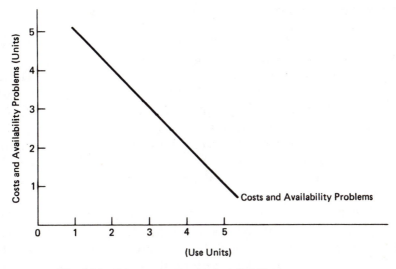

Fig. 14-1. Computer costs and availability versus use.

to support a "resource" than an expense. We are seeing, and will continue to see, more emphasis on this concept, and support by top management for the various functions of personnel. From a purely economic sense, it is one of the areas that management now is starting to recognize as a major contributor to the bottom line.

Coupled with this are the new reporting relationships we are starting to see for personnel. Personnel or human resources directors are starting to report at the top of the organization. It is anticipated that this will continue to increase as the human resource concept expands and is recognized for its true value.

The costs and availability of computers are going to allow more areas access. Service centers have sprung up around the world. An individual can have access to a major computer by paying a nominal rental fee. Small mini- and microcomputers are entering the market, even now, and make the concept of personnel having its own computer even more feasible.

These changes indicate that everyone in personnel will have almost complete computer availability in the future. This will be true regardless of the size of the organization. This means that more systems will have an automated base.

PERSONNEL SYSTEMS

The classic organization chart of personnel will probably be changing. Even today, most major organizations have a personnel systems department or division that reports to the head of personnel. The size of these will probably expand as their importance increases. All organizations will see such groups reporting at the same (or higher levels) than compensation, employment, etc. (This is shown in Fig. 14-2.)

The value of having proper personnel systems in place is only starting to be recognized. Proper systems more than pay for themselves. Improper or malfunctioning systems are the cause of a major portion of today's personnel operating problems.

This is being recognized by most major organizations, since sheer size forces their attention to systems problems. They then set up and develop people to deal with the personnel systems problems. The word "develop" is used here because the present environment does not produce formally trained people in this area as it does, say, in compensation.

As colleges and universities recognize this need, more courses will appear in the area of personnel systems. Organizations won't have to "grow their own," but will be able to draw on a formal pool available in the marketplace. This will be significant, since formal training and development will result in even further refinement of the art of personnel systems.

MANAGERS' ROLES

Tomorrow's managers will be more comfortable with computer systems and automation in general. These managers are in the "pipeline"

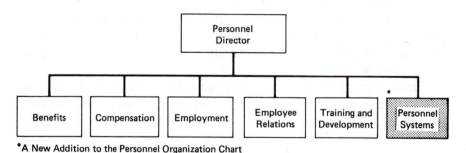

*A New Addition to the Personnel Organization Chart

Fig. 14-2. Personnel systems: A major organization entity.

of today's schools and colleges. Automation is not only present, but is often used as part of class projects, and to solve various problems and assignments. They are developing a comfort level that will carry over into their future work.

The same is occurring with systems concepts. A systems approach is no longer isolated or limited to the scientific area of study. It is prevalent in the business, psychology, and law schools, where many personnel people are trained. This will also have a carry-over into the business world.

The situation just mentioned is shown in Fig. 14-3. Those managers who have not received formal exposure in the school system aren't as likely to use such concepts on the job. The exception to this would occur if training and development occurred after the person started in the job market.

PERSONNEL SYSTEMS NEEDS

From the technical point of view, the future needs of personnel are known today. This is true at least in the near future (of, say, five or ten years). Hardware and software will be positioned to meet these needs (Fig. 14-4 reflects these requirements).

The needs shown in Fig. 14-4 are a representation, not an exhaustive list. Each personnel area has its own unique requirements. Obviously,

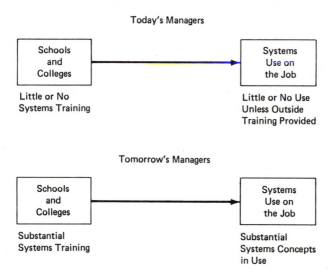

Fig. 14-3. Importance of training and development in systems.

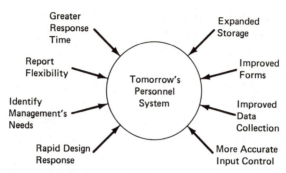

Fig. 14-4. Personnel system needs. (The future needs of personnel are identical to those of today. Hardware and software will just be in a better position to meet them.)

it is impossible to address all of these here. We can, however, explore some of the major ones noted in Fig. 14-4.

Going clockwise in the example, we might start with expanded storage. Personnel generates a great deal of information on individual employees. This ranges from basic location data (e.g., department, employee number, shift), through payroll data (e.g., salary, hours worked, overtime), and onward to skills inventory data (e.g., education, experience, preferences).

The list of personnel storage needs is almost infinite. Most organizations have needs for hundreds of data elements for each individual. As an organization has grown, this has created storage problems, particularly for computer-based systems.

Each generation of computer systems seems to provide for greater storage capacity. Even today, the problem for personnel is not as critical as it was a few years ago. Technology breakthroughs that could provide almost unlimited storage are more nearly approaching fact than fantasy. This may no longer be a problem tomorrow.

Improved forms were noted, too, as a requirement. We often don't recognize the importance these play in the life of any system. Forms are frequently input- or data-capturing documents, as well as the output media.

Technology has had an impact on forms in the past, and will continue to do so in the future (for example, on the development of forms that produce copies without carbon paper and on the design of turnaround documents). The use of the CRT (Cathode Ray Tube) or television image of a form is another innovation coming into greater use. This has encouraged the idea of a paperless use of forms. An electronic image for viewing, typing onto, etc., which is both used and filed via the electronic media.

The use of color is now possible on a CRT, and it provides many opportunities for the future. A form can be displayed, and specific areas to be filled in can be color-coded for ease of completion. Error messages can be flashed in attention-getting colors if an entry isn't allowable based on the review of an internal table file. The future uses are only limited by one's imagination.

Improved data collection techniques will be available in the future. Particularly when a system or a portion of one is being set up, initial data capture is of major concern. Obtaining accurate information to establish a base can be a major undertaking. This is even more of a problem when the data is in manual form and must be collected such that it can be in an acceptable format for a computer.

A number of things are transpiring in this area of data collection to make the future a little easier. First, many data sources have been, or are being, converted to machine-readable formats. Thus, the data is already available in a useful format, and reduces the collection time normally experienced in a conversion effort. Secondly, where systems are manual, there are more experienced people around to handle the collection and ensure that data is converted for automated use. In other words, the knowledge of how to do this, which once had to be achieved by trial and error, is now there.

More accurate input will result as new devices assist in data collection. Putting CRTs in the field, where the changes are actually occuring, is one method which is now being used more frequently. On-line data capture and change capability is expanding in use.

Department stores and supermarkets update their inventory records now through on-line systems at the check stands. Banks are establishing similar systems, both through terminals placed with the tellers, and the entire concept of automated teller machines.

More accurate input control is one of the spinoffs of this occurrence. Reducing the amount of paper and the number of hands it must pass through, by its very nature, reduces the potential for error. The more a transaction can be simplified, and the fewer people it has to pass through to enter the final record, the more accurate it will be (this is shown in Fig. 14-5).

Rapid design response is shown as another item we can anticipate in the future. This will be the result of not only the advances in technology, but the wider acceptance of personnel systems as a major function within the personnel department. It often takes years to identify a needed systems change and then get someone to go through the steps to get it into place.

Part of this problem is the learning that must take place by those in the organization who may be untrained in personnel systems. They often go through trial and error solutions, and these are time-consuming. A well-trained and well-staffed personnel systems group will help in expediting these changes.

Another area that will aid in ensuring more rapid systems design is the ever-increasing capability and availability of outside consultants and vendors. Personnel systems are being recognized as a market for these services. Those personnel departments that want a system change rapidly put into place will have the option of buying this and having it installed.

Identifying management's needs is another item that will show improvement in future personnel systems. It was noted earlier that the technical aspects of systems and the hardware were given special attention. Information was designed to satisfy the programmers and analyst involved. The real users (management) were often overlooked.

It was frequently assumed that management would become interested and learn to adapt or learn the more technical aspects. This has not been the case in most instances. The systems must bend to pro-

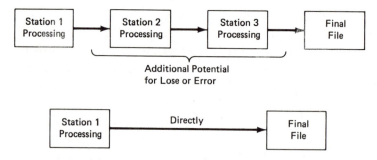

Fig. 14-5. Reducing processing steps reduces error.

vide information that management needs in a format that is usable to the layman.

The early systems analysts had visions of each manager having his/her own terminal. The manager would be able to type inquiries and interact with the computer. This has never occurred to any great degree. Where such a system has existed, it has usually been ignored by management, and ultimately abandoned as being too complex.

This has been particularly true in personnel. Managers in this area are normally not "numbers people" or computer-oriented. Systems have to be provided that supply the information without intimidating the user. Most analysts are now aware and more sensitive to this issue. Future systems will be provided with greater attention to these types of needs, for those that do not meet them are useless.

Report flexibility is another item we will see more and more emphasis on. Output requirements are not static. Everything is changing at an accelerated rate, and report requirements are no exception. Few, if any, reports in the personnel area can exist for more than a couple of years without being changed.

Many reports are obsolete before a change can be processed. There is a need to change reports almost with each new production run. The answer is flexibility in being able to format both the individual reports, and the data elements to support them.

What is needed in personnel is to change reports without going through a lengthy approval process. The answer lies in who has the control to make this change. If this control is with the user, the needed priority can be assigned. However, if the control is with a third party, other department's priorities may take precedent.

The trend is for user control of this portion of the automated system. Personnel will have greater flexibility based on this. It will speed up the responsiveness to the ever-changing environment.

This leads to the concept of greater response time and use by management. (Fig. 14-6 depicts this.) Management will rely on personnel and its related support systems only if these are responsive and timely.

If management needs to know the average salary rate for employees, the number possessing degrees, the average accumulated sick days, etc., it is usually to solve an immediate problem. The information must be available in a timely manner, and not two weeks or a month after it is requested.

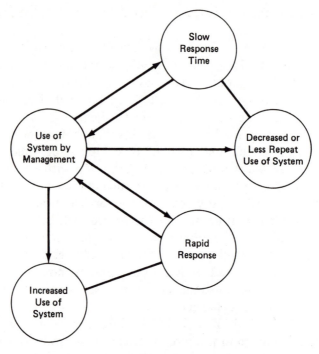

Fig. 14-6. System response time.

When the response time is too long, management will have to make an arbitrary estimate or postpone the solution. How fast should the response time be? This will vary with each individual problem; however, the target should be a matter of minutes.

This target will raise some eyebrows, particularly those who are used to responding in days or weeks. It is hoped that it also raises the conscious level of these individuals. Data that is a day old or weeks old is often of little use. The response time to meet most management requests is much shorter.

One way advanced personnel systems groups are meeting this demand and short time frames is anticipating management's questions in advance. Going into the field and surveying key managers produces very rewarding results. This can lead to a preparation of a ready reference information report on salient personnel data. Another way is the use of variable on-line data retrieval systems, which can be formulated to list the data elements, accumulate totals, etc., on the data in which management is interested. Future personnel systems will aim at these types of response methods. In doing so, management, at all levels, will use them more and be attuned to the value of timely human resource data.

LEGAL DICTATES

Figure 14-7 shows an area of future concern. Changes in laws regarding human resources increase the requests on personnel and the requirements to respond. This, in turn, takes an ever-increasing chunk of corporate or organizational resources to respond.

It is doubtful that any of the existing laws that were reviewed in a previous chapter will be repealed. This, by itself, has made all aspects of personnel more complex and the need for a systems approach mandatory. Even the existing laws and regulations in the United States have not been fully interpreted as to their impact.

Each court decision sets another precedent or a new wrinkle in what an employer must do, is not allowed to do, or is liable for if it happens in the workplace. These interpretations normally go against the employers and for the employee. Each one increases the burden on the organization; hence, it increases the burden on personnel.

There is no reversal of this trend on the horizon. Even as existing laws age and lose their sting, they are replaced by others. Most firms

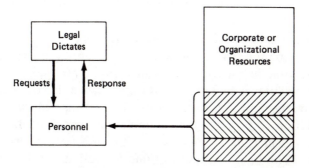

Fig. 14-7. Impact of legal dictates. (Changes in laws regarding human resources increase the requests on personnel and the requirements to respond. This, in turn, takes an ever-increasing chunk of corporate or organizational resources to respond.)

have to set in place detailed procedures for hiring, firing, and day-to-day interface with an employee. Added documentation is a requirement for almost any personnel action — not just to handle complaints from unions, but those from individuals as well as class action suits from groups.

Preparing this documentation to protect against litigation requires fairly detailed systems. For example, individuals used to be fired when management felt they were no longer of use to the organization. The employee left, and that was the end of it if no union was involved.

Today, that has changed, and it will continue to change even more in the future. Employees (particularly women and minority employees) have substantial recourse through any number of government agencies. In many areas, there is no charge whatsoever for these services to the employees. The employer involved must bear the costs of answering any charges in full. Even if the organization protests, the courts tend to support the individual against the organization. This means that before an organization takes action that may upset the employee, a complete documentation package justifying such action must be established. This takes time and requires a very specific procedure to ensure that the action is applied uniformly to all employees.

The trend of employees taking action against employers is on the increase. There are several reasons for this. One is increased availability of government agencies and special interest groups to ensure employee rights. Another is increased awareness by employees that have recourse. As cases are won by employees, these are spread, not only by word of mouth, but by the newspaper and television, especially where substantial awards or new issues are involved.

The legal community is involved in representing both sides. This area is growing in numbers as night schools provide an increasing number of people trained in law. Recent changes have allowed attorneys to advertise in the United States. This means wide dissemination of information to both employees and employers. This fact by itself will definitely provide an increase in litigation on matters related to personnel. The liabilities and options for action will be announced through the various advertising media.

The concepts of work, jobs, and professions are changing. Recently, the concept of property rights has come into play regarding an employee's job, and extending this, we may see people having the same rights to employment as they do to their homes, stocks, autos, etc. Depriving a person of employment may be similar to foreclosing on a mortgage or repossessing a car.

Societies place a high value on what people do. What they make, where they work, and *if* they are working or are unemployed are significant factors in how an individual is judged. Most people are judged by their work. The "property rights" concept may have a very firm grounding or foundation when viewed in these terms.

Regardless of your position on an employee's rights to employment — and this can be an emotional issue — the impact will be significant. Personnel will be upfront with regard to the future activity in this area. Because of this, personnel will need substantial information and support systems to adequately perform.

IMPACT ON BOTTOM LINE

The concept of personnel becoming a profit center is an interesting and very real possibility. In the past, we have always viewed personnel as being "burden," "overhead," or an item of "expense." As noted in previous chapters, things have occurred which have somewhat altered our view of this activity, and may continue to alter it in the future.

The various laws and regulations, such as affirmative action, OSHA, and ERISA, have made organizations, both large and small, aware of their vulnerability in this area. Large organizations have increased their personnel staffs, and are frequently having the director of personnel report at the very top level. Small organizations are going out and hiring key personnel professionals, where a clerk or secretary used to operate a recordkeeping or low-keyed personnel-related operation.

Why? Probably not for any altruistic reason, but for hard, cold economic reality. The organizations are now becoming increasingly subject to suits, fines, and assorted legal actions based on the handling or mishandling of personnel matters. A single manager or supervisor by some unintentional act may subject an organization to millions of dollars of suits, claims, etc.

This is staggering, and the threats of it happening are on the increase. Small firms may be even more threatened, because a substantial suit might put them in jeopardy of being financially insolvent. A good personnel department is starting to be viewed as an insurance policy.

Organizations are starting to view this as a mandatory cost of doing business — a form of liability insurance in the people sector.

This aspect of the bottom line impact is starting to produce other trends, which we may see more of in the future. (This is shown in Fig. 14-8.) It should be noted that a "strengthened personnel department" is only one of the reactions taking place. The emphasis has been placed on it in this book because it is the major topic or area of discussion.

However, there are many reactions outside of directly strengthening personnel. These will have, in some cases, both a direct and an indirect effect on the personnel function. Organizations, if they are to survive, must take steps to protect themselves. The greater the threats of potential negative actions, the more and varied will be the reactions.

Looking past personnel in the figure just noted, we see multiple present and future occurrences. Political action is one which can be and is exercised. If the laws become to oppressive, organizations must take steps to have them modified or nullified. Not doing so is like hitting yourself over the head with a hammer. We will see more activity in the political action area in the future.

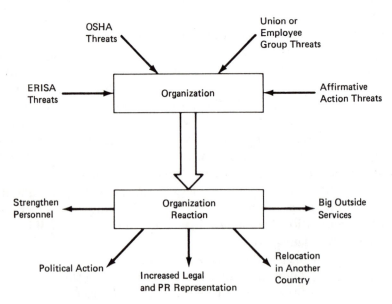

Fig. 14-8. Personnel-related threats or problems.

Personnel is not alone on the front line. Legal and public relations groups are being hired to come to the aid of organizations. Since it is often through legal action that organizations are being challenged, they must defend themselves in the same way.

Many organizations do very positive things for employees that are not recognized. These are often taken for granted or overlooked, while negative occurrences are trumpeted all over. A public relations department or outside firm can aid in this area. We will continue in the future to see more effective organizations turning to this resource. The value of proper communications will continue to get the recognition and use it deserves.

Relocation in another country, where restrictions are less severe, is another fact of life. The availability and type of labor force is a decision all organizations face. More organizations are multinational both in practice and in attitude. The basic laws of economics indicate they will gravitate to areas where the most efficient and cost-effective resources are available — and this includes the human resources.

The concept of buying outside resources has long been in use. More firms are turning to this in an effort to reduce their personnel problems. More organizations are maintaining a small cadre of experienced professionals and not hiring or increasing their staffs. Those services that are needed and can't be produced inside are purchased from the outside vendors, consultants, agencies, freelance workers, etc.

As stated, this very effective technique is not new. Organizations that wish to remain non-union have used it for years. If an activity became unionized (e.g., janitorial service, warehouse facilities), these were sold, and the service then purchased.

The small cadre (or nucleus) idea seems to be catching on. The larger the organization, the greater a target it becomes for personnel problems of all types. Many organizations have found that they can grow in the scope of their activity, while staying small in the number of staff.

OVERALL TECHNOLOGY

Earlier in this chapter, we focused on one aspect — computers. Technology cuts across a wide spectrum, of which computers are a part. The human resource is one element in this equation. More emphasis will be placed on evaluating its worth in the future. A great deal of effort will be placed on identifying what individual people are worth to an organization. What does Bill or Mary actually contribute? What do we lose or gain if he/she is no longer with us?

This type of measure is certainly available in the sales area and on the production line. It has been missing in the staff, administrative, and management areas. A concerted effort has to be made to fully identify and quantify these areas.

This will allow more work to be handled by automation. When the cost/contribution factors can be measured, a valid management decision can be made. This does not mean dire consequences for the workforce. Nothing is sacred about a forty or fifty hour workweek, as was previously noted. It can easily be three or four hours, with more leisure time and other options going to the workforce.

Technology in all its forms can be an aid to social and economic development on all fronts if applied properly. Regardless of whether we accept this statement or not, rapid technological advances are on the way. Those who recognize and accept this will be in a much better position to work with (rather than against) and truly manage the change that is coming.

15
SUMMARY AND CONCLUSION

The material in this book was developed with practical application as its goal. It should be of use to those managers and practitioners in the field who are involved with personnel or human resources. It has been designed to aid all the areas of personnel (e.g., employment, training and development, compensation, benefits, and employee relations).

As was indicated, there is a definite trend to establish a "personnel systems" department or division as part of the main personnel function. This will, it is hoped, provide some help and guidance in this area. This is a relatively new and pioneering aspect of the personnel function when compared with the more classical activities. It is, however, rapidly appearing in all major personnel activities.

Though it is not written in the traditional academic format with multiple quotations and references, scholars in the management and personnel field may find it of distinct interest and use. It is written from many years of practical experience designing and developing systems in all areas of personnel. There is no real substitute to actually having performed an activity and experiencing the results.

As personnel systems are taught in the classroom, this may serve as a text or reference guide. We are starting to see this area achieve a separate entity. In doing so, formal programs of training and development have started to appear in greater numbers. This practical guide may aid them in their efforts.

The task of personnel or human resources management is not limited to the personnel department. Managers in all areas have the responsibility for people. The chapters in this book should give managers at all levels a logical or systems approach to dealing with the personnel activity.

SEQUENCING

Particular attention was given to the order and sequencing of the chapters. Those reading the entire book will find there is a continuity to the chapters and a meaning to their order. However, individual chapters are titled to assist those who are interested in only a specific area or portion.

The book starts out describing the steps in developing a personnel system. As part of this, a personnel system is defined. Then, the activity of developing a system overview and a system specification is reviewed.

As part of the initial chapters, the concepts of obtaining management and employee support are explored in some detail. No system should be designed for the use or satisfaction of the analyst or designer; the management and employees of the organization must live with, and use, the personnel system on a daily basis, and their involvement and support are critical both to proper design and proper use later on. This is a key ingredient that is too often overlooked.

Manual systems are explored because they also have a very real place. All personnel systems are not computer-based. Even those that are have a substantial number of manual support systems. Consequently, every personnel system, even the most highly automated, makes use of some of the manual applications.

The chapter on manual systems explores the manual or machine (computer) decision-making process. Guidelines are provided to aid in this decision. There are places where, and times when, automation is appropriate and others where it is not. Prolonging the decision to automate when it is warranted can cause problems. Simultaneously, automating for the sake of automation can be a problem when a manual system is more cost-effective.

The timing of the decision to automate a certain area of the personnel system or systems is also explored. Many organizations wait until problems have reached the crucial stage before changing their methods. This can be both disruptive and costly. Change and growth should be timely and controlled to create the least disruption possible.

Computer systems have significantly affected personnel. Many types and combinations of manual/machine systems were discussed. In many instances, neither stands alone. Combinations of manual/

machine or automated systems are the rule rather than the exception. Most automated systems, as previously noted, are intertwined with manual systems.

Determining a computer system that fits the organization involved is an important issue that was covered. Coupled with this is finding a system that truly fits management's needs. No system that does not fit both the needs of the organization and its management will successfully survive.

Portions of the system that lend themselves to automation were reviewed. Portions that are not candidates for automation were also covered. One of the main considerations is not to automate for the sake of automation, but only when it is truly justified on a cost/use basis.

The legal aspects of personnel systems was discussed in a separate chapter. It was also reviewed in applicable sections of other chapters. A great deal of emphasis was placed on this because of the wide-ranging impact it has had on the personnel area in the United States. Probably no single item has had such a significant effect on personnel in recent years.

Many of today's personnel systems in the United States do not exist by choice, but were required in order to deal with various legal aspects of personnel. Originally, it was the unions and related legislation that concerned personnel. Now this has been broadened by the legal implication of such issues as affirmative action, ERISA, and OSHA.

One of the major points in this chapter dealt with the fact that this activity is on the increase. Personnel departments need to have flexible systems that can respond very rapidly to change. Even as the present laws become outdated they will be replaced by other issues. The interpretation of the laws frequently change, adding new and additional requirements. There frequently is not a long response time provided. Organizations are required by law to respond within a certain time, and the existing systems must be able to meet this need.

Defining the data elements is given a separate chapter. Too many personnel systems are designed by starting with the existing reports as a base. It is proposed here that the data elements and not the reports are the important factor.

Data elements, on the other hand, if properly identified and defined, handle today's needs and are the basis for tomorrow's. Selecting the proper data elements allows us the flexibility to change and modify future reports as changing requirements dictate. It is the establishing of a good data element base that allows for future flexibility. This flexibility ensures that the system does not become obsolete at too rapid a rate.

In setting up a data element base, the importance of using all the organization's resources is stressed. Management has input to offer, but because of the broad nature of their work, they frequently don't have all of the details. The importance of including the employees in this part of the analysis is stressed. Properly combining the input both of management and the employees is the real objective.

The chapter on defining the reports points out that the existing reports are probably already historical or obsolete. Most systems are designed or redesigned because the older ones are not meeting the needs. This means that although the existing reports may be a reference point, they should be viewed with extreme caution. We probably don't want to duplicate a substantial number of them in the future system.

Since new reports should be a product of the new or revised system, the sources for definition are crucial. Obviously, just as with data elements, management and the employees constitute one source. Additionally, we may want to look at what other related organizations are doing. Others have probably confronted similar problems, and we may be able to benefit from their experience.

The chapter on forms in very salient, since these provide both the input and frequently the output to both manual and automated systems. Questions that are addressed include the number of forms and ways of reducing if too many are found. Frequently, the number of forms in an organization will grow. Setting up a forms control system often just drives the organization into the use of "bootleg forms." Forms are there to meet an operational need, and when the systems aren't meeting them, other means (e.g., bootleg forms) will be used.

A certain amount of time was devoted to discussion of the "turnaround" form concept. Here, the form is designed to serve as both an input and output document. Advantages to this concept include saving time in completing forms, reducing the number of forms needed, etc. With the ease of computer printing of documents, we are seeing more use of this concept.

The concept of distributed data processing, and the idea of user control was discussed. Placing input and output devices in the hands of the user creates additional possibilities for reduction in forms. If nothing else, fewer people will have to handle the forms and this alone should speed up processing and reduce lost documents.

A chapter was devoted specifically to the make or buy concept. This area, similar to legal considerations, shows up throughout the book. This is as it should be, since make or buy is one of the most important options and considerations in personnel both today and tomorrow.

Almost everything we do in personnel can be done inside or purchased from an outside vendor/consultant. There are multiple cost considerations that can affect the bottom line. Even the smallest firm can have the most sophisticated personnel system in a given area, if they are willing to pay the price.

There are many trade offs involved in this area. Buying a system provides out of pocket costs, but can reduce payroll in the long run. Also, time is a consideration and a purchased system can be up and running in a much shorter time frame (frequently, weeks or months, where a system that is designed internally may take years). Security is a concern that some express regarding a purchased system; however, it was pointed out that it may not be as large a concern as we so often hear voiced.

Employment systems are explored in detail, the first step being to identify what the possible parts or functions are. Employment is seldom viewed as an area where system techniques are applicable. This is a myth that has caused a great deal of disorder and chaos to surround the activity.

Because of this, a series of definitions for this area seemed in order. Effort was taken to define and show examples of a recruitment and selection system or systems. The same treatment was given to recruiting and interviewing support systems.

The legal aspects of testing were reviewed and explored. Testing as part of the selection procedure was almost totally abandoned at one time due to affirmative action concerns. Now, with properly validated tests, we are seeing a reemergence of this useful tool.

The concept of human resources and the possible return on investment was briefly explored. Proper recruiting and selection can actually save money. The name of the game is to match the proper person with the right job. When this is not done, a loss is incurred. From the positive point of view, when the match is successful, a gain occurs.

Training and development is another chapter covering the classical personnel activities. The parts of a training and development system are discussed in detail. Also, the definitions of what constitutes training and what constitutes development are covered in some detail. These definitions have often been a past problem, and it was felt clarification was in order.

The importance of fully tracking both internal and external training and development was stressed. This sets the stage for a training and development or instructional audit. It is felt that this is a critical activity. With so many dollars and so much time devoted to instruction, it is imperative that we develop concrete measures.

A properly designed instructional audit provides these measures. They allow us to determine which courses were effective in meeting the organization's needs, and which were not. It is only through such efforts that we can ensure that the programs are cost-effective. Without such an audit, we are only guessing.

Various training and development resources were explored. A very wide choice is available in the marketplace. Courses can be purchased which are canned or individually tailored. Instructors, as well as the whole range of media, are available for purchase or rent. It was pointed out that one of the big problems is making a selection from such a wide range of choices.

The importance and involvement of line management was stressed. There has been rather traditional conflict as to who would have control over the activity — the line or the training and development staff. They both have a great deal to offer to the process. The line user has technical expertise in the work area, as well as on-the-job experience. The training and development staff has specialized knowledge in the instructional area. The key is in combining the two and working toward the end objective.

The parts of a compensation system were reviewed. Probably no other area in personnel has the systemized base that compensation does. Most areas in a well-run compensation operation have a strong systems base and operate in a well-ordered manner.

The importance of surveys as part of a compensation package was stressed. It is through surveying that an organization can compare its activities with others. Most organizations operate in multiple markets for the human resource. It is important to identify and define these markets.

Definitions and descriptions of job classification structure, job descriptions, job specifications, and job analysis were given. It was stressed that job specifications systems seem to be on the increase, the primary reason being that job specifications use measurable criteria as their base. This makes them difficult to establish, but more valuable to those involved.

The concepts of merit and promotion were discussed. It is important that an organization develop a definition that truly separate the two. Too frequently, this area is left fuzzy or undefined. The definition is important to equitably reward and motivate those in the organization.

Organization structure and analysis were reviewed under the compensation heading. Frequently, the structure is an important factor in determining both responsibilities and level of pay. A proper organization structure aids in wage and salary administration.

The parts of a benefits system were reviewed. A few years ago, benefits would have been part of the compensation chapter. Today it warrants a chapter of its own. Benefits has been one of the more recent growth areas in personnel. In many organizations, the number of people dedicated to it exceeds the number assigned to other personnel activities.

Cost of benefits are increasing at a wild rate. This "hidden payroll" may exceed the actual payroll in the near future. Even if no new benefits are added, the costs of the existing ones will contine to escalate. One of the largest ones is medical coverage, and there is no end in sight for cost increases in this area.

Cafeteria-style benefits are becoming popular. Here an employee selects the benefits that are most appropriate to his/her individual situation. Some people may need dependent coverage for medical, while others may want an expanded retirement system. The requirements in this area will vary with lifestyle, family size, age, etc. In reality, no individual benefit plan, except the cafeteria type, can meet the different needs.

As in many personnel systems, there is an option to go to an outside source to purchase the service. This option has been available for a long time in the benefits area due to the time-proven support from the various facets of the insurance industry. Many firms opt to use some of the excellent outside services available in the benefits area, and keep the size of their internal staff small.

The security question was explored. By its very nature benefits involve third parties for claims processing, payments, etc. Laws regarding disclosures of information have to be closely watched and followed. Benefits can be vulnerable in this area, and it is only through continuous vigilance and proper systems management that trouble can be avoided.

Employee relations and research systems were outlined. Employee relations frequently stands as a separate entity. However, in recent times, research as an active area in personnel has started to come into its own. It is often attached to the employee relations activity, since the information it produces is often used here.

One technique that is frequently used in this area is attitude surveys. Finding out how the employees feel about a certain subject (e.g., rate of pay, benefit package, etc.). This can be useful information, but there can be some danger in obtaining it. Those questioned (the employees) are going to want to know the results. Then they are going to want to know what action has been taken to resolve areas identified as problems. Management may not be ready to spend the money or take the specific action to change the situation. This survey technique is useful, but has its drawbacks if immediate corrective action can't be delivered.

Providing management with proper statistical data can produce positive results. Management needs statistical data on human resources to adequately plan as well as to answer employee inquiries. One of the areas employee relations should concern itself with is ensuring that proper and complete information is available to management.

A great deal of information that is of a general nature, such as rate ranges, is often maintained as confidential or restricted. One of the questions that confronts every employee relations activity is the determination of which data is to be restricted. Systems design in this area presents some interesting and challenging alternatives.

A great deal of attention is paid to the recordkeeping activity. Probably even more attention is being paid to this now that employees are allowed by law to see their personnel files or records. Certain aspects of the personnel recordkeeping system have been automated; however, the manila folder is still actively used for keeping individual employee files.

The last chapter in the series was the future of personnel systems. It was emphasized that what we do in the present actually creates our future. There is no real mystery, since we can see the changes taking place today that will pretty much dictate what activities will be occurring in tomorrow's personnel systems.

One thing that we are seeing is the increased availability of computers and related automated equipment. In the past, personnel and other administrative functions had to wait in line to use the equipment — if they were scheduled at all. Today, almost anyone can have access to a large computer through a rented terminal if need be.

Personnel systems groups are starting to be recognized as part of the personnel function. Most large organizations have them, and the smaller ones soon will as well. Personnel systems will be recognized as part of the classic organization structure.

The legal control that we see today is not going to diminish. Organizations will continue to take steps to protect themselves through strengthening the personnel department, legal resources, public relations, etc. Other countries may assume a competitive edge, and some United States firms may take work out of the country because of complex personnel related regulations.

Management is going to focus more on the bottom line from a people perspective. Efforts are going to be intensified to measure productivity — particularly in the administrative areas. A great deal of attention will be paid to putting a dollar value on the human resource. This is one series of systems that has been talked about in the past, and will now receive the attention needed to bring it into active use.

INDEX